# NAFTA AT TWENTY: ACCOMPLISHMENTS, CHALLENGES, AND THE WAY FORWARD

# HEARING

BEFORE THE

## SUBCOMMITTEE ON
## THE WESTERN HEMISPHERE

OF THE

# COMMITTEE ON FOREIGN AFFAIRS
# HOUSE OF REPRESENTATIVES

ONE HUNDRED THIRTEENTH CONGRESS

SECOND SESSION

JANUARY 15, 2014

## Serial No. 113–112

Printed for the use of the Committee on Foreign Affairs

Available via the World Wide Web: http://www.foreignaffairs.house.gov/ or
http://www.gpo.gov/fdsys/

U.S. GOVERNMENT PRINTING OFFICE

86–298PDF                 WASHINGTON : 2014

For sale by the Superintendent of Documents, U.S. Government Printing Office
Internet: bookstore.gpo.gov   Phone: toll free (866) 512–1800; DC area (202) 512–1800
Fax: (202) 512–2104   Mail: Stop IDCC, Washington, DC 20402–0001

## COMMITTEE ON FOREIGN AFFAIRS

EDWARD R. ROYCE, California, *Chairman*

CHRISTOPHER H. SMITH, New Jersey
ILEANA ROS-LEHTINEN, Florida
DANA ROHRABACHER, California
STEVE CHABOT, Ohio
JOE WILSON, South Carolina
MICHAEL T. McCAUL, Texas
TED POE, Texas
MATT SALMON, Arizona
TOM MARINO, Pennsylvania
JEFF DUNCAN, South Carolina
ADAM KINZINGER, Illinois
MO BROOKS, Alabama
TOM COTTON, Arkansas
PAUL COOK, California
GEORGE HOLDING, North Carolina
RANDY K. WEBER SR., Texas
SCOTT PERRY, Pennsylvania
STEVE STOCKMAN, Texas
RON DeSANTIS, Florida
TREY RADEL, Florida
DOUG COLLINS, Georgia
MARK MEADOWS, North Carolina
TED S. YOHO, Florida
LUKE MESSER, Indiana

ELIOT L. ENGEL, New York
ENI F.H. FALEOMAVAEGA, American
  Samoa
BRAD SHERMAN, California
GREGORY W. MEEKS, New York
ALBIO SIRES, New Jersey
GERALD E. CONNOLLY, Virginia
THEODORE E. DEUTCH, Florida
BRIAN HIGGINS, New York
KAREN BASS, California
WILLIAM KEATING, Massachusetts
DAVID CICILLINE, Rhode Island
ALAN GRAYSON, Florida
JUAN VARGAS, California
BRADLEY S. SCHNEIDER, Illinois
JOSEPH P. KENNEDY III, Massachusetts
AMI BERA, California
ALAN S. LOWENTHAL, California
GRACE MENG, New York
LOIS FRANKEL, Florida
TULSI GABBARD, Hawaii
JOAQUIN CASTRO, Texas

AMY PORTER, *Chief of Staff*      THOMAS SHEEHY, *Staff Director*

JASON STEINBAUM, *Democratic Staff Director*

————

## SUBCOMMITTEE ON THE WESTERN HEMISPHERE

MATT SALMON, Arizona, *Chairman*

CHRISTOPHER H. SMITH, New Jersey
ILEANA ROS-LEHTINEN, Florida
MICHAEL T. McCAUL, Texas
JEFF DUNCAN, South Carolina
RON DeSANTIS, Florida
TREY RADEL, Florida

ALBIO SIRES, New Jersey
GREGORY W. MEEKS, New York
ENI F.H. FALEOMAVAEGA, American
  Samoa
THEODORE E. DEUTCH, Florida
ALAN GRAYSON, Florida

# CONTENTS

# NAFTA AT TWENTY: ACCOMPLISHMENTS, CHALLENGES, AND THE WAY FORWARD

---

## WEDNESDAY, JANUARY 15, 2014

House of Representatives,
Subcommittee on the Western Hemisphere,
Committee on Foreign Affairs,
*Washington, DC.*

The subcommittee met, pursuant to notice, at 2:36 p.m., in room 2172, Rayburn House Office Building, Hon. Matt Salmon (chairman of the subcommittee) presiding.

Mr. SALMON. A quorum being present, the subcommittee will come to order.

I will start by recognizing myself and the ranking member to present our opening statements. And without objection, the members of the subcommittee can submit their opening remarks for the record.

Now I yield myself as much time as I may consume to present my opening statement.

Good afternoon, and welcome to this hearing to evaluate the North American Free Trade Agreement. About 20 years ago, we passed this I think wonderful piece of legislation and entered into this agreement, and just last month, the subcommittee held a hearing in my home State of Arizona on our commercial relationship with Mexico and what we can do to better facilitate the flow of commerce along our southern border.

So today's hearing on NAFTA is an appropriate follow up to that hearing, this time looking more broadly at our trade and investment relationships with both Canada and Mexico, the strengths and the weaknesses of NAFTA with 20 years behind us, and what needs to be done now to improve upon this agreement.

I want to thank Chairman Royce for his leadership. I believe he will be joining us at the hearing today. We had a little vote that interrupted everything on the floor. I apologize to our panelists.

Mr. DREIER. On the rule, I noticed.

Mr. SALMON. On the rule, yes, and you know how important that is, the former Rules chairman.

It seems clear to me that America's leadership in promoting free trade policies has been a vital part of American prosperity. The level of competition created by free trade policies has been the impetus for remarkable innovation. While leading to the opening of exciting new markets around the world, at home this has allowed the American people to access more varied goods and services at lower prices, while creating jobs, a practical and positive effect for free trade that benefits every American.

American leadership in promoting free trade agreements globally has been instrumental in the spread of economic freedom and the rule of law worldwide and has spurred unprecedented economic growth in the developing world. Indeed, free trade has proven to be the most important tool of U.S. foreign policy seeking to promote individual liberty and economic freedom around the world. The world isn't entirely free yet, but the message of economic freedom and the power of entrepreneurship is being spread to far away corners of the globe thanks to American leadership and free trade.

Twenty years ago, NAFTA was a truly groundbreaking agreement, becoming the first regional trade agreement between two developed countries and a developing country.

There was a lot of controversy surrounding NAFTA then, and even today, it would be misleading to conclude that NAFTA was a perfect agreement. No trade agreement ever is. What it did do, though, was to integrate the U.S., Canadian, and Mexican economies, resulting in what today is a $19 trillion regional market.

Indeed, figures from the United States Chamber of Commerce suggest that a combined total of 14 million U.S. jobs depend on trade with Mexico and Canada. Canada is the United States' largest export market and our most important supplier of energy. Meanwhile, it is worth noting that Mexico imports more U.S. goods than all of Latin America combined and more than Brazil, China, India, and Russia combined.

NAFTA reduced and eventually eliminated trade barriers, leading to a generation of impressive growth in trade and investment among the three countries. This resulted in production sharing made possible by proximity between the three economies by integrating and strengthening supply chains in key industries. What this means for the United States is that imports from Mexico contain 40 percent U.S. content and imports from Canada contain 25 percent U.S. content. By way of comparison, imports from China contain only 4 percent U.S. content.

Despite the reassuring promising numbers, we will likely hear from some of our witnesses, now that NAFTA is 20 years old and all grown up, we have an obligation to take a critical look at the agreement and find ways to make it even better.

I have always been a firm believer in free trade and positive effects of truly free trade. That is exactly why right now, as negotiations are underway to liberalize trade through Transatlantic Trade and Investment Partnership, TTIP, and the Trans-Pacific Partnership, TPP, is exactly the right time to look at NAFTA, figure out where it helped U.S. businesses and commercial interests and the interests of American consumers and families, and where the agreement may have failed us.

As we learned during our field hearing on trade facilitation with Mexico, 20 years into NAFTA should be the time we recommit our resources to border infrastructure by identifying new approaches to financing and commercial partnerships so we can make the investments necessary to make cross-border commerce more efficient and streamlined without neglecting legitimate security concerns. The U.S. should partner with and press Mexico to continue addressing the insecurity that plagues Mexico while reforming and updating its judicial system.

While NAFTA certainly improved our commercial relationship with both Canada and Mexico, the treaty needs to be able to address 21st century trade challenges. One of these challenges is intellectual property rights protection issues that persist with our Canadian neighbors. In 2013, the USTR designated Canada as a watch list country on its special 301 report. This is a pending issue between our Nations, and I hope we can resolve it soon to ensure that individuals and companies have transparent legal avenues to ensure ownership and profits for their innovations.

Further, it is important to note that there is only political support for these trade and investment agreements as long as people follow the rules, and the rights of innovators and investors are protected. It is notable that the North American energy independence and security was conspicuously absent from original NAFTA negotiations. At the time, Mexico had a constitutionally closed energy regime, making its inclusion impossible.

Today Mexico is engaged in implementing serious energy reform that will open its energy sector to foreign investment through a constitutional amendment they are—in fact, they recently passed, promising to increase Mexican oil production and make North American energy independence a reality.

Sadly, today, the roadblock to realizing energy security and independence in North America has been put up by the Obama administration right here in the United States. I once again call on the administration to finally approve the Keystone XL pipeline, which would be a job creator and an important part of our energy security for this country. Continued obstruction not only threatens the environment as less secure modes of transportation are utilized, but it sends a negative message to our Canadian partners and allies.

I want to thank Ambassador Carla Hills and my friend former Congressman David Dreier for testifying on our first panel, and Mr. Eric Farnsworth, Mark Elliot, and Dr. Duncan Wood for joining us on the second panel to discuss the North American Free Trade Agreement, the accomplishments, the challenges, and the way forward.

I look forward to a productive hearing.

I would now recognize the chairman of the full committee if that is all right with you?

Mr. ROYCE. No, I think we should go to Mr. Sires.

Mr. SALMON. Okay. Let's go to Mr. Sires then.

Mr. SIRES. Thank you, Mr. Chairman.

Good afternoon, and thank you to our witnesses for being here today.

It has been 20 years since the North American Free Trade Agreement between the United States, Mexico, and Canada came into force. The trade agreement was a staggering scope and spurred vigorous and contentious debates in each country and houses of government. Proponents predicted the creation of countless U.S. jobs alongside the deterrence of foreign undocumented immigrants. Opponents, on the other hand, foresaw the opposite. The agreement aimed to eliminate virtually all tariffs on trade between partner countries over a 15-year period. In the process, NAFTA created the largest trade bloc in the world of its kind.

Ultimately, although the agreement has served as a template for subsequent trade agreements, NAFTA has not lived up to the entirety of expectation espoused by its advocates, nor has it resulted in the catastrophic losses predicted by its opponents.

There is no denying that in terms of trade alone, NAFTA has achieved impressive indicators. U.S. trade with NAFTA countries has more than tripled to over $1 trillion a year. Trade barriers have been eliminated, supply chains enhanced, opportunities for investments increased, and mechanisms for trade dispute resolutions were established.

In 1993, the U.S. trade has increased over 500 percent with Mexico and over 190 percent with Canada. The United States is Mexico's largest trading partner and the largest foreign investor. Mexico, in turn, is the third largest U.S. trading partner after Canada. Together, Mexico and Canada accounted for 32 percent of total U.S. exports in 2012. These statistics are telling, but they speak little of the broader implication least accentuated by the agreement.

NAFTA was comprehensive but far from complete, let alone harmless. For one, labor and environmental provisions were both weak and separate from the core of the agreement. Additionally, there has been little convergence in terms of economic growth, income disparity, job creation, and regulations, in part because the agreement attempted to integrate two advanced, developed countries with a developing country that was ill ready to absorb the collateral damage of trade liberalization.

This was especially true for Mexico, whose NAFTA advocates hoped the agreement would help them export goods, not people, when in fact the opposite occurred. As Mexico shifted away from agriculture, rural populations were pulled northward because of the weak job creation in Mexico and the demand for migrant workers in the United States.

Meanwhile, in Canada and the United States, job losses were numerous in sectors such as manufacturing, as the new economic model exposed firms to greater competition. On the other hand, NAFTA cannot take sole responsibility for the various changes in trade, labor, environment, or various economic occurrences that have taken place amongst partner countries since 1994.

Unforeseen global events, like the 9/11 terrorist attack and the global financial crisis of 2008, played a role. For Canada and the U.S., the agreement enhanced an already existing free trade accord, while for Mexico, the agreement provided an international treaty mechanism to solidify and expand existing domestic reforms.

Today, there is talk of revisiting the agreement. The human and the economic costs are far too great to ignore this task. Tensions remain between border security and trade facilitation that affect the flow of goods, services, and people across the border.

Of particular concern to me and countless New Jersey-based life science companies is Canada's unfortunate record of protecting intellectual properties through its discriminatory use of the so-called ''promise'' doctrine. The doctrine stipulates that the utility of a patent must be first demonstrated or predicted at the time of the patent application. This makes it easier for generic companies to challenge the usefulness of a patent drug and ultimately launch a parallel generic brand.

This case is not just a matter of fairness but about more than 50,000 workers employed by 1,700 New Jersey-based life science companies that have invested more than $8.7 billion in research and development and created more than 72,000 jobs, spin-off jobs in New Jersey, and contributed nearly $27 billion to the New Jersey economy in 2012. That trading is economic reality of globalization does not justify ignoring unintended and direct consequences on the environment, workers, and private enterprise. As stewards of the world's largest economy, it is our duty to be mindful of this reality as future agreements come to the forefront. At the same time, lesser developed countries must recognize that large trade agreements are not substitutes for national development policies.

Twenty years under NAFTA has made it clear that the agreement was both oversold and greatly underestimated. Furthermore, assessing the agreement's impact as an outright success or failure is far too narrow and simplistic.

I look forward to hearing from our panelists and thank you very much.

Mr. SALMON. Thank you.

I would like to recognize the chairman of the full committee, Mr. Royce.

Mr. ROYCE. Thank you, Mr. Chairman.

Chairman Salmon, I just want to thank you for the field hearing you held recently and for chairing this today, very successful field hearing, and it is a pleasure to see my former colleague, David Dreier, who did so much on the issue of advancing trade, along with our very successful former Trade Representative.

Carla, it is good to see you, Ambassador, here with us as well.

I think there is a great potential for increased trade in this hemisphere. And within North America, I think we could do a lot to boost our exports and create jobs here and not only in North America, as a matter of fact, but also in the Pacific as well. We have a key destination there for manufacturing goods from the U.S. All along that rim of the Pacific, and the Trans-Pacific Partnership agreement I think is important to that end.

I think, and this was the subject of Mr. Salmon's hearing, but I think that requiring better management across our borders is key to some of this, and our business group reports that risk management, improvements in infrastructure, a focus on travel and trade facilitation, that this can have a sort of symbiotic advantage in advancing not only our economic interests but also protecting our security interests at the same time. I think repairing and upgrading ports that have become a little dilapidated, a little deteriorated, closing underutilized facilities, extending the hours of overcrowded entry points, all of these things can, I think, assist and, frankly, are absolutely necessary.

So, today, the United States is overtaking Russia in terms of our capacity at energy production, top oil and gas-producing Nation in the world in short order here I think, and Canada and Mexico are our top sources of importation of petroleum at this time into the U.S., so clearly, the other issue here is greater energy cooperation with our neighbors, which again, our goal at the end of the day is to have the cheapest energy costs in the world and not to have our economic competitors have that advantage, and so the affordability and availability of natural gas has the potential here of revolutionizing North American manufacturing. As you drop that cost down, it is amazing how energy has become in many ways the most important component; energy and labor are the most important components now for light manufacturing, and today, the U.S. I think has an opportunity also with Canada.

Since 2008, the Canadians have been pushing hard on an agreement that has been on the President's desk for the Keystone XL project. The Canadians are not going to wait around forever, and they have made it clear to us the pipeline is going to be built; the question is whether it goes south or whether it goes west, and if it goes west, that oil is going to be shipped to our economic competitor, China.

They are going to develop that resource one way or the other, and I think further delays on the final decision at Keystone will probably mean that the U.S. will be the loser in this, and we will have lower energy costs eventually coming from our economic competitor, who will be the beneficiary of the fact that we have turned down something that economically made all the sense in the world.

Since I think the ratio is about three-quarters of what we—of what Canadians spend with the profits end up to be to buy manufactured goods from the United States. They are on our border. I mean, you think about the issues with respect to energy security. All of these demands are focused on Mexico and Canada here with respect to energy going forward.

So I thank you all, and again, I thank the chairman for conducting this hearing today.

Mr. Sires, thank you, too, for your engagement on these issues.

Mr. SALMON. Thank you.

The chair will recognize Mr. Meeks for a brief statement.

Mr. MEEKS. Thank you, Mr. Chairman, and Mr. Ranking Member.

Over the years, I have worked with many of today's witnesses on finding ways to make pending U.S. trade agreements increasingly stronger, and in that regard, my friend and former colleague David Dreier was certainly an able partner. It is good to see him and all of you here today, and today, I hope we can combine a look back at NAFTA with a look ahead at how we might enhance the gains and learn from any mistakes.

A couple of years ago, the Center for Global Development released a paper with the title, ''Why is Opening the U.S. Market to Poor Countries So Hard?'' In posing that question, the CGD highlighted the role that trade has played globally in lifting millions of people out of the ranks of poverty. I mention that question on this occasion because I want to start by noting a very important but often overlooked point in the debate about NAFTA's success or failure.

The agreement was between two developed and one developing nation at a time when that was not a popular nor easy thing to do. If it is still challenging today to get developed nations to enter into meaningful trade agreements with developing nations, then certainly doing so 20 years ago was monumental.

President Clinton was courageous in championing what he knew would be a difficult but important trade deal for America. NAFTA was good for Mexico at a time when its economy and democracy was tumultuous. The agreement was forward looking for the United States. We had a choice. We could have sat back as a Nation and yielded to the controversy and opposition to NAFTA, but we chose instead to go ahead of globalization trends.

So we solidified rules of trade with two critical trading partners and in so doing ensured that we would have a fair chance to increase the exporting of U.S. goods and import in ways that would enhance our production and international supply chain.

While there are winners and losers in any trade relationship and economic shift, NAFTA did not turn out to be the great job killer that opponents expected nor did it do as much as some of the enthusiasts expected.

Lastly, let me just pivot for a few points that are particularly important to me as a Representative from the State of New York. Since 1993, New York exports of merchandise to NAFTA countries have grown by 123 percent. Merchandise exports from our State to Canada were at $15.4 billion in 2012 alone. These numbers demonstrate why New York is one of the 40 States that hold Mexico or Canada as their top trading partner. When I consider the totality of circumstances, I am convinced that both critics and enthusiasts made NAFTA better and continue to force improvements in the way we negotiate trade agreements.

As I see it, TPP and TTIP are important opportunities to build upon the lessons of NAFTA, and I look forward to the perspective of our panelists, look forward to continuing to work with you, Mr. Chairman.

Mr. SALMON. Thank you, Mr. Meeks.

Pursuant to committee rule 7, the members of the subcommittee will be permitted to submit written statements to be included in the official hearing record.

And without objection, the hearing record will remain open for 7 days to allow statements, questions, and extraneous materials for the record, subject to the length limitation of the rules.

Mr. SALMON. I would like to introduce the first panel.

Ambassador Hills is chairman and chief executive officer of Hills & Company International Consultants. She also served in the Cabinets of President George H.W. Bush as the United States Trade Representative and of President Gerald R. Ford as Secretary of the Department of Housing and Urban Development. Currently, she serves as a member of the Secretary of State's Foreign Affairs Policy Board. She graduated from Stanford University and obtained her law degree from Yale Law School.

And next I would like to introduce David Dreier. During his more than three decades of congressional service, Mr. Dreier was a champion of enhanced trade liberalization between the U.S. and all of its global partners, but especially its North American neighbors. He introduced the first legislation calling for NAFTA and worked closely with Presidents Bush and Clinton throughout its negotiation and passage through Congress. He helped make the case for deepening ties with Canada and Mexico. He formed the House Trade Working Group, which not only was instrumental in the passage of NAFTA but continued to be a driving force in ushering every subsequent trade agreement through the House, including CAFTA and the FTAs with Colombia and Panama. He is the chairman of the Annenberg-Dreier Commission, which seeks to foster deeper connections and economic growth in nations of the Pacific Rim, including North, Central, and South America, Asia, and the greater Pacific.

And so, with that, I would like to recognize Ambassador Hills.

But before I do recognize you, I am going to explain the lighting system in front of you. You will each have 5 minutes to present your oral statement. When you begin, the light will turn green. When you have a minute left, the light will turn yellow. When your time has expired, the light will turn red. I ask that you conclude your testimony once the red light comes on.

After our witnesses testify, all members will have 5 minutes to ask questions, and I urge my colleagues to stick to the 5-minute rule to ensure that all members get the opportunity to ask questions.

Ambassador.

### STATEMENT OF THE HONORABLE CARLA A. HILLS, CHAIRMAN AND CHIEF EXECUTIVE OFFICER, HILLS & COMPANY INTERNATIONAL CONSULTANTS

Ambassador HILLS. Thank you, Mr. Chairman, and thanks, members of the committee.

It is an honor for me to appear before you and particularly with David Dreier, former chairman of the House Rules Committee and one of the greats who served this body. His efforts were instrumental in securing the approval of the North American Free Trade Agreement, the NAFTA, and as noted, it was the first comprehensive free trade agreement to join developing and developed countries. It achieved broader and deeper market openings than any prior trade agreement negotiated anywhere in the world, and as a result, economic activity among the three nations exploded.

Today, Canada is America's single largest export market. More than 8 million jobs depend upon our exports to Canada. And Mexico is our second single largest export market, and some 6 million U.S. jobs depend on our trade with Mexico.

Over the past two decades, a highly efficient and integrated supply chain has developed among the three North American economies. More than $2 billion worth of goods and services cross our northern border every single day and while roughly $1 billion per day crosses our southern border.

Specialization has boosted productivity in all three economies. We not only sell things to each other, we make things together, and quite remarkably for every dollar of goods that our two neighbors sell to us, there are 25 cents worth of U.S. Inputs in the Canadian goods and 40 cents in the Mexican goods. By way of comparison, with respect to our imports from China, that is 4 cents.

And most of those who have complained about the NAFTA focus on Mexico, but the economic data proves that having Mexico as a NAFTA partner has served U.S. interests extremely well. Last year, roughly 14 percent of our total exports went to Mexico, and as the chairman pointed out, that is more than all of our sales to the rest of Latin America. NAFTA, our exports to Mexico have grown two times faster than our trade to the rest of the world, and that is true of Canada as well.

Although some contend that the NAFTA has depressed wages, a recent study by economists at Yale and our Federal Reserve concluded that wages, when adjusted for inflation, have actually risen as a result of the NAFTA in all three countries, and it is widely agreed that the NAFTA's market opening increased jobs connected to exports, which pay between 15 and 20 percent more than jobs that are purely domestically focused.

With 116 million consumers and a purchasing power of over $1 trillion, Mexico offers significant opportunity to U.S. entrepreneurs, large and small, but smaller enterprises in particular benefit from Mexico's proximity and openness to our trade because Mexico purchases about 11 percent of the exports from small- and medium-sized businesses, which account for more than half of our Nation's job creation.

In short, the NAFTA has made our region one of the most competitive in the world, but the rest of the world has not stood still. Increasingly, trade agreements where the United States is not a party give entrepreneurs from other countries preferential access to key markets that our entrepreneurs don't have, and there are a number of actions that we could take, the building on the NAFTA platform, that would create new commercial opportunity, cut costs, and create jobs, and let me mention quickly just three.

First, the Trans-Pacific Partnership. In 2012, Mexico and Canada joined the United States and eight other nations to negotiate the TPP to link Asia and Pacific. There are eight bilateral trade agreements between the three NAFTA governments and the other TPP participants that were negotiated after we negotiated the NAFTA. Their differences in rules of origin and custom procedures add costs to our trade which could be dealt with in the TPP.

Second, the Pacific Alliance is an ongoing trade negotiation initiated by Mexico, Peru, Colombia, and Chile in 2011. Last year, Costa Rica gained approval to join. Mexico and Canada are observers along with seven other nations. Canada and the United States, having them join the alliance could eliminate costly regulatory differences among the three nations.

And thirdly, a North American-European trade agreement. Last year, the United States and the European Union's 28 states launched a Transatlantic Trade and Investment Partnership. Our average tariffs are quite low. The real potential for boosting economic growth will come from reducing the maze of regulatory standards covering a long list of goods and services. Enlarging this agreement to include our two neighbors, which already have separate trade agreements with the European Union, would greatly reduce costs and complexity of trade. Of course, the infrastructure is a very big issue. The United States could address that.

I am grateful to the chairman and members of the committee for the opportunity to share my thoughts on the NAFTA and moving forward and how we can build upon it, and so I thank you and look forward to your questions.

[The prepared statement of Ambassador Hills follows:]

## STATEMENT OF THE HONORABLE CARLA A. HILLS
### Chair & CEO of Hills & Company, International Consultants
### U.S. Trade Representative 1989-1993

### Before The House Committee on Foreign Affairs
### Subcommittee on the Western Hemisphere

### Wednesday, January 15, 2014

### "NAFTA at Twenty, Accomplishments, Challenges, and the Way Forward"

Mr. Chairman and members of the Committee, thank you for inviting me to share with you my views regarding the North American Free Trade Agreement ("NAFTA") signed by President Herbert Walker Bush in 1992, approved by the U.S. Congress and signed into law by President Clinton in 1993, and entered into force in 1994. With 20 years of experience it is timely to ask what the NAFTA has accomplished and consider whether it has significance for the future.

In making these assessments, it is important to be clear about what the agreement actually did. By joining the economies of Canada, Mexico and the United states, the NAFTA created a $19 trillion regional market with 470 million consumers. It was the first comprehensive free trade agreement to join developed and developing nations. And it has served as a template for our subsequent trade negotiations for it achieved broader and deeper market openings than any prior trade agreement anywhere in the world by:

- Eliminating tariffs on all industrial goods;
- Guaranteeing unrestricted agricultural trade between the United States and Mexico;
- Opening a broad range of services including financial services and provided national treatment for cross border service providers;
- Providing a high standard of protection for patents, trademarks, copyrights, and trade secrets, and the first international trade agreement to do so; and
- Establishing clear rules to protect the rights of investors by prohibiting barriers such as local content restrictions and import substitution requirements.

As a result of the market openings created by the NAFTA, economic activity among the three nations exploded. Today Canada is America's single largest export market, and it sends us roughly 98 percent of its total energy exports making it our largest source of energy products and services. More than eight million U.S. jobs depend on our trade with Canada. Mexico is our second single largest export market, and some six million U.S. jobs depend on our trade with Mexico.

Over the past two decades a highly efficient and integrated supply chain has developed among the three North American economies. Intra-regional trade flows have increased roughly 400 percent from roughly $290 billion in 1993 to over $1 trillion in 2012. More than $2 billion in goods and services cross our Northern border each day, while roughly $1 billion per day cross our Southern border.

About half our trade with Canada and Mexico takes place between related companies, and the resulting specialization has boosted productivity in all three economies. We not only sell things to one another, we make things together.

Quite remarkably for every dollar of goods that our two neighbors export to us, there is 25 cents worth of U.S. inputs in the Canadian goods and 40 cents in the Mexican goods. By way of comparison, with respect to our imports from Japan the U.S. input is 2 cents and with respect to China it is 4 cents.

As a result of the NAFTA, cross border investment with our two neighbors has soared as well. Canada has invested over $200 billion in the United States which makes it America's fifth largest investor, while the United States has invested roughly $310 billion in Canada to become its largest investor.

Mexico also has made substantial investments in the United States since the signing of the NAFTA in such sectors as cement, bread, dairy, and retail, which have contributed to our tax revenues and jobs. U.S. investment in Mexico has grown substantially as well, about half of it in the manufacturing sector, particularly in the auto sector. Much of the output from our investments in both Canada and Mexico comes back to us as imports of intermediate goods which adds to our competitiveness in the production of the finished product.

In spite of this very substantial intra-regional economic growth that can be traced to the NAFTA's opening of regional markets, the agreement has its critics. Most of those who attack the NAFTA on economic grounds focus on Mexico, not Canada. They claim that the partnership is one sided: that the NAFTA is Mexico's gain and America's pain. But the economic data proves that having Mexico as a NAFTA partner has served U.S. economic interests extremely well.

Last year roughly 14 percent of our nation's total exports went to Mexico, exceeding our sales to Brazil, Russia, India, and China, all of the "BRICs" combined. Indeed Mexico buys more U.S. goods than all of the rest of Latin America combined, and more than Germany, France, Great Britain and the Netherlands combined.

Although some contend that the NAFTA has depressed wages, a recent study by economists at Yale University and the Federal Reserve concluded that wages when adjusted for inflation have risen as a result of the NAFTA in all three countries. Also it is widely agreed that the market openings created by the agreement generated a substantial increase in jobs connected to exports, which on average pay 15 to 20 percent more than jobs that are purely domestically focused.

With 116 million consumers and a purchasing power of over $1 trillion, Mexico offers significant opportunity to U.S. entrepreneurs large and small, but smaller enterprises in particular benefit from Mexico's proximity and openness to our trade. Mexicans purchase about 11 percent of the exports from our small and medium size enterprises, which account for more than half of our nation's job creation.

Even Mexico's exports to others benefit the U.S. economy because of their high percentage of U.S. content and the fact that for every dollar that Mexico earns from its exports worldwide, it spends 50 cents on U.S. goods.

The economic integration that has occurred among the three North American nations in the two decades since the NAFTA took effect has made North American region one of the most competitive in the world. But the rest of the world has not stood still. Countries and regions around the world are becoming more competitive. Supply chains encircle the globe, and increasingly bilateral and regional trade agreements where the United States is not a party are giving entrepreneurs from other countries preferential access to important markets that our entrepreneurs do not have.

Continuing to open global markets to products, services, investment, and ideas originating in North American and ensuring that our supply chains work at maximum efficiency is vital to our nation's continued growth and competitiveness.

Building on the NAFTA platform, there are a number of actions that we could take that would create new commercial opportunity, cut costs, create jobs, and generate substantial economic benefits for all our citizens. Let me mention three.

First, the Trans-Pacific Partnership. In 2012 Mexico and Canada joined the United States and eight other nations to negotiate a Trans-Pacific Partnership ("TPP") to link the Asia and Pacific regions. Having our two neighbors at the table will better enable us to take positions to maintain and advance the unique competitiveness of the North American Region. It also gives us an attractive opportunity to address issues that were not relevant when the NAFTA was negotiated, like data flows and advanced telecommunications.

It also provides an opportunity to harmonize a number of conflicting trade rules that plague our entrepreneurs. Today there are eight existing bilateral trade agreements between the three NAFTA governments and other TPP participants that were negotiated after the NAFTA came into being. These eight agreements have different rules of origin, custom measures, and other border red tape that add costs and complexity to both the import and export of goods. These differences could be dealt with in the TPP agreement.

Second, the United States should consider joining the Pacific Alliance. After the NAFTA was signed in 1992, leaders in the Western Hemisphere enthusiastically talked about a free trade hemisphere by 2005, which never happened. Today, we could join an effort to restart the process.

The Pacific Alliance is an ongoing trade negotiation initiated by Mexico, Peru, Colombia and Chile in 2011. Last year Costa Rica gained approval to join. Mexico already has separate bilateral trade agreements with the four governments as do Canada and United States. Seven other governments have been granted observer status including Canada and the United States.

The stated goal of the Pacific Alliance is to create free trade among its members on a step-by-step basis. It seeks to create free trade with based on existing bilateral trade accords. The

Framework Agreements specifies that governments seeking to join must have existing bilateral trade agreements with current members. Having all of North America be part of the Alliance would shrink transaction costs by eliminating regulatory differences and set an example for the rest of the hemisphere and beyond.

Third and most importantly, a North American-European Union Trade Agreement. Last year the United States and the European Union's 28 states launched a comprehensive Trans-Atlantic Trade and Investment Partnership ("T-TIP"). The third round of negotiations occurred this past December.

Without question the T-TIP is a very big deal. Together the United States and the European Union account for more than half the world's GDP, 40 percent of global trade, and 80 percent of global capital markets. Our two way trade in goods and services tops $1 trillion supporting 13 million jobs, and our two way investment is nearly $4 trillion. Roughly half our total foreign investment goes to E.U. member states and 62 percent of the E.U.'s total investment comes to the United States.

Apart from our tariffs on agriculture, textiles, apparel, and footwear which are relatively high, our average tariffs are quite low, around 3 percent. The real potential for boosting economic growth will come from reducing the maze of different safety and regulatory standards on a long list of goods from automobiles to pharmaceuticals.

With respect to automobiles for example the European Union and the United States have a long list of different safety mandates that include lights, door locks, brakes, seats, seat belts and electric windows. Constructing separate manufacturing facilities to respond to these differences is costly. Mutual recognition that the divergent standards provide an equivalent level of safety would very substantially reduce the complexity and costs.

Even larger gains could be obtained through harmonization or mutual recognition of various rules that govern services such as engineering, finance and telecommunications. Making these rules more compatible and less cumbersome would greatly reduce the costs and complexity of doing business both across and on both sides of the Atlantic Ocean.

The European Centre for Political Economy estimates that a broad agreement that eliminated the remaining tariffs between the European Union and the United States and harmonized or mutually recognized different regulatory approaches could add $126 billion to the U.S. economy per year, $157 billion to the E.U. economy and $134 billion to the global economy.

The projected benefits are far more likely to be realized or enlarged by including Canada and Mexico. Enlarging the T-TIP to include our two neighbors would very substantially boost the benefits for all the participants in a number of ways.

First, it would strengthen the agreement by adding 150 million consumers and $3 trillion in GDP expanding market opportunities and providing a golden opportunity to improve regulatory coherence with respect to more than half the world's trading volume.

Second, failure to include all three North American economies would substantially add to the complexity of doing business across the Atlantic. That is because Mexico has had a free trade agreement with the European Union since 2000, and this past October Canada announced that it had successfully concluded one. Having to deal with three separate agreements with different rules of origin and custom measures would create a headache and an unnecessary cost burden for entrepreneurs on both sides of the Atlantic.

Third, failure to include Canada and Mexico in T-TIP would erode the unique and hugely beneficial economic integration that we have achieved with our two neighbors as a result of the NAFTA. Since the NAFTA took effect two decades ago, an integrated supply chain has developed among the three North American economies that is truly unique. Intra-regional trade flows are up more than 400 percent. Having different regulations and standards for the three North American partners would substantially erode the efficiencies derived from the NAFTA.

And finally it could facilitate President Pena Nieto's program of economic reform that is opening sectors of Mexico's economy like energy and telecommunications. Pointing to the benefits that Mexico could potentially obtain from joining this mega-agreement that involves more than half of global GDP could help him build political support for his proposed economic reforms that we strongly support.

As we move forward in this 21st century, we need to take steps to maximize our competitiveness and productivity that will bolster future economic future growth. That will require the three NAFTA governments, along with their universities, think tanks, and business organizations to educate their respective populations about the tremendous benefits that can result from thinking about and dealing with trade and investment opportunities not only as single nations but also as the highly integrated region that North American has become. There is no better time than the 20th Anniversary of the NAFTA to start the process, and I am grateful to the Chairman and members of this Committee for this opportunity to share my thoughts.

————

Mr. SALMON. Mr. Dreier.

### STATEMENT OF THE HONORABLE DAVID DREIER, CHAIRMAN, ANNENBERG-DREIER COMMISSION AT SUNNYLANDS

Mr. DREIER. Thank you very much, Mr. Chairman.

I was talking to one of our great diplomats yesterday who, when I said I was going to be testifying with Carla Hills before your subcommittee, Mr. Chairman, he described her as a force of nature, and not long ago, I was talking to someone else about Carla Hills, and this woman said she is a national treasure.

You didn't have everything in that introduction. She was the first woman to be the Secretary of Housing and Urban Development, the fourth woman to serve in a President's Cabinet, and she has roots in California, which even though I no longer represent California, I am always pleased to be in her presence. And I will say that when I think back about my involvement, I was little more than a foot soldier in the George H.W. Bush, Carla Hills, Bill Clinton, Mickey Kantor struggle to make sure that we succeeded with the North American Free Trade Agreement.

It is particularly poignant for me, Mr. Chairman, to be here, and I will say that I don't have too many regrets of my service, but one of them was that I wasn't able to serve with you again. I campaigned with you in the last election, I know, but I worked closely with you on this issue of trade, and I know you feel passionately and strongly about it, and I appreciate that, but I am sorry we weren't able to serve together.

I also have to say that it is great to see Mr. Sires. As I said in the anteroom, we worked very closely on the Colombia-U.S. Free Trade Agreement, and I appreciated his activism and support there, and also I want to say that I appreciate the concerns he raised in his opening statement as well.

And Gregory Meeks has been my partner in crime for a long period of time on virtually every trade agreement, and he has stepped up, often facing criticism within his party, and he has done it because he knows and believes it is the right thing to do.

And I have to say to Mr. Duncan and Mr. DeSantis and Mr. Radel, it is nice to see you all, and I hope very much that you will focus attention on this issue because it is so important.

I have to say, Mr. Chairman, this is the first time that I have been back to the U.S. Capitol since January 2nd of last year, which is when I had the opportunity to manage the floor debate for the special rule on the fiscal cliff legislation, and by virtue of being the floor manager, I took the opportunity to offer some advice, and that is why it is particularly poignant for me to be invited to be here on this occasion, because in the last speech that I gave on January 2nd, the day before Ambassador Hills' birthday, I will say that I talked about the need for bipartisanship, and I talked about the issue of trade as creating a very unique and important opportunity for us to do just that.

And that is why I am very gratified to see that while we had this bipartisan effort put together with President George H.W. Bush and President Clinton, and as I said Ambassador Hills and Ambassador Mickey Kantor and others within both administrations who worked very strongly on this, I am particularly pleased to see that we are today working for a broader bipartisan effort on this.

And I want to congratulate Chairman Royce for the very strong statement that he made in support of something that we have yet to discuss, and that is trade promotion authority. It seems to me that as we look at the imperative of moving ahead with all of these agreements, it is going to be absolutely essential that we give the President of the United States the opportunity to negotiate. Now, I know there is some who have raised concern about trade promotion authority, believing that somehow this transfer of power to the President.

When Carla Hills was United States Trade Representative, I will tell you that during the negotiations of the North American Free Trade Agreement, she did because she understood the imperative of consulting with the United States Congress, and she did that consistently, and other USTRs have done that as well. Why? Because they know that this institution has the power to vote yes or no on those agreements.

And so I do believe that moving ahead with TPA and maintaining the right that the Congress has to defeat a bad agreement is clearly there, although I believe that virtually any opportunity that we can reduce the barriers to the free flow of goods, services, capital information, ideas, and people is a very important thing for us to do.

As you mentioned, Mr. Chairman, for the last year, I have had the opportunity to chair a commission. I am happy that Ambassador Hills serves on the advisory board along with Mack McLarty and Jon Huntsman and Henry Kissinger and Madeleine Albright of our commission, which really grew from the vision that Ambassador Walter Annenberg had.

When Ambassador Hills was negotiating the North American Free Trade Agreement in the late 1980s and early 1990s, Ambassador Annenberg was sitting at his home at Sunnylands, and he was talking about the fact that the future is around the Pacific. Mr. Chairman, nearly two-thirds of the global GDP and nearly two-thirds of the global population is around the Pacific, and by virtue of that, I truly believe and you as a westerner understand that, as opposed to these guys from Jersey and New York, understand full well that that is in fact the wave of the future.

We have a tendency here in New York and Washington to focus across the Atlantic. We have a wide range of entities that do that, and it is true TTIP will in fact be the largest free trade agreement in the history of the world, but I suspect that TTP may be completed before it, and until TTIP is put into place, the Trans-Pacific Partnership, now that Japan is part of that, will be the largest free trading bloc in the history of the world.

It seems to me that that vision that was put forth by Walter Annenberg is one that was very, very prescient, and I am pleased to be utilizing his estate at Sunnylands for a wide range of meetings. The Presidents of China and the United States met there last summer, and I am hoping very much that we will be able to do things like include leaders within the Pacific Alliance there, and so I have lots of things that I could go through.

I want to talk about the changes that have taken place in Mexico. One figure I was just given yesterday is did you know that as we look at the new Mexico, yes, poverty and the disparity in income levels is a very important thing, but Mexico now is part of a very important partnership on the Learjet, Canada, United States, and Mexico, all countries involved in that process, and guess what? Mexico last year graduated more engineers than the United States of America did, and so this perception of Mexico is one that needs to change. And I think that as we mark this 20th anniversary, Mr. Chairman, it is very, very important for us to do everything we can to focus on how we can address these concerns. The answer to the problems of NAFTA is more NAFTA.

Thank you very much.

Mr. SALMON. Thank you very much, Mr. Dreier.

[The prepared statement of Mr. Dreier follows:]

DAVID DREIER
CHAIRMAN, ANNENBERG-DREIER COMMISSION

HOUSE COMMITTEE ON FOREIGN AFFAIRS
SUBCOMMITTEE ON THE WESTERN HEMISPHERE

"NAFTA at Twenty: Accomplishments, Challenges, and the Way Forward"

January 15, 2014

Mr. Chairman, Ranking Member Sires, thank you for your leadership on this important and timely topic and for giving me the opportunity to offer remarks.

For the last year I have had the privilege of leading a commission based at the Annenberg Foundation's Sunnylands Trust, charged with helping to carry on the bold and prescient vision of Walter Annenberg. When the North America Free Trade Agreement was being negotiated over two decades ago, Walter Annenberg was articulating the philosophical underpinnings for the agreement. He was a great believer in our potential as a nation that engages proactively and productively with our neighbors and partners. Though our tendency here in Washington has long been to focus our gaze eastward across the Atlantic toward Europe and the Middle East, Walter Annenberg, from his home at Sunnylands in Rancho Mirage, CA, cast his gaze westward across the Pacific and southward to Latin America.

We passed NAFTA because we knew it was important to our interests to strengthen our partnerships with our two closest neighbors. We knew if we could leverage our respective strengths, we would grow more, and be better able to compete globally. And, we knew how important growth and competitiveness would be to America's security and wellbeing in the very different world that was then dawning.

The 20th anniversary of that historic agreement is a good moment to look back and assess its achievements and its shortcomings. But it matters a lot more for us to use this moment to look forward, draw the right conclusions, and lead.

That's an opportunity for Democrats, Republicans, the Congress, the White House, and the private sector. What is the future of America's role in the worldwide marketplace and how can our North American partnerships be a force multiplier in this role?

NAFTA was revolutionary two decades ago, but we at the threshold of even greater opportunities today. That is why the last two administrations have pursued a broader vision. Today our strategic stake in an ever-greater flow of goods, services, capital, information, ideas, and people dramatically exceeds anything imaginable when NAFTA was implemented. The rise of China, and other big emerging economies, has fundamentally altered the landscape of the worldwide marketplace.

The fundamental question today, as we reflect on NAFTA, is much bigger than how to increase trade among the U.S., Canada, and Mexico. The big challenge is to build and leverage a North

American economy that becomes a platform for leadership and growth in the broader global economy, spanning the Pacific and Atlantic Oceans.

We need to harness the power of our combined workforces, energy resources, innovation, and investment to create the world's most successful global competitor. To create a 21st century partnership that drives unparalleled growth, job creation, widespread prosperity, and creative solutions to the shared challenges we face.

Our NAFTA partners are integral players in the drive to conclude what will be the biggest, most ambitious, highest-standard free trade agreement in the world, the Trans Pacific Partnership. Our efforts--all of our efforts--to meet TPP's requirements will effectively update, upgrade, and strengthen NAFTA.

Presidents Obama and Peña Nieto and Prime Minister Harper have all expressed enthusiasm for building on NAFTA's solid foundations--and taking steps that strengthen the platform as we reach more boldly across the Pacific and Atlantic. Secretary Kerry further articulated the Administration's view in his excellent address to the OAS late last year. All signs point to a productive trilateral discussion when our three leaders meet in February.

Mr. Chairman, today's hearing is timely. There is a ripe opportunity for Congressional leadership to help secure our economic wellbeing for generations. Trade has always been politicized. But I am encouraged at the resurgence, in the last few years, of bipartisan support for trade liberalization. I can think of no other initiative with a bigger potential payoff in terms of human opportunity, economic growth, and America's global competitiveness. As elusive as bipartisan cooperation has often been, we have a tremendous opportunity for a Republican House, a Democratic Senate, and President Obama to work together. Progress on virtually every major challenge we face as a nation -- from security to immigration to jobs to energy -- can be enhanced through a stronger, more vital North American economy and workforce, competing in a growing global economy. I commend the Subcommittee for the important work it is conducting and encourage you to seize this opportunity to look forward and think boldly as you contemplate and assess NAFTA's first 20 years.

For many years it has been fashionable, at home and abroad, to talk about American economic decline. But that view is just false. America is not in economic decline. Yes, we have challenges. As we address them, investors all over the world continue to bet massively on our economy. That's not because of sentimental reasons. It is because they smell success and opportunity.

We are at the start of what could be one of the most remarkable periods of growth in our history. Revolutions in energy and food production, transformational new technologies, good North American demographics, and a resilient culture of innovation, create amazing new possibilities. American manufacturing, once written off by many, is on the rise.

But nothing is inevitable. We are well positioned to benefit dramatically from the world that is emerging-- provided we are wise enough to support policies that favor that. And provided we lead in shaping a world where economic growth can beget human opportunity and spur collaboration on big global challenges.

Our global leadership -- of which NAFTA is a prime example -- has helped get us to the inflection point we're at today. Continuing to lead on trade, perhaps more than on any other issue, may determine how the promise of the 21st century plays out for our people and the world.

Thank you Mr. Chairman.

Mr. SALMON. Ambassador Hills, I received a surprisingly large number of calls from many organizations and companies expressing concerns with Canada's inconsistent IPR protection and enforcement.

As you may know, last year, Canada remained on USTR's watch list because many American companies still face legal uncertainty during the administrative process to obtain IPR protection. How can we confront the issue, and how can we ensure that our trading partner doesn't institutionalize bureaucratic barriers for our companies?

I am also concerned that some of the worst offenders of IPR violations globally would be India and China, and how do we stress to them the importance of fixing those problems if a developed nation such as Canada continues to deal with our IPR issues in the manner that it does? I am a strong supporter of NAFTA, but I think this is an issue we have got to address because it is hurting a lot of our companies that are doing business in Canada.

Ambassador HILLS. I agree that intellectual property protection is absolutely essential. We are on the up scale in terms of our production, but even in great families, you have differences, and we do have differences with Canada, as they do with us.

The remedy is to sit down and work through it. It is certainly made easier by reason of having a trade agreement that sets out the rules so that you have a mechanism of addressing and getting a solution to the rules, so we have a lot of positive, many, many more positive with our first largest trading partner or single largest, and some negatives, and they have a few complaints about us.

Mr. SALMON. I am sure that is true. I think we would like to explore any and all opportunities because I think globally it is more important than just our bilateral relationship. I think it portends to influence a lot of our other relationships on IPR with other nations.

Mr. Dreier, did you want to comment on that?

Mr. DREIER. Well, the only thing I would add to that is we have a process in place to deal with this, and that was really part of this whole negotiation. And, you know, when you are dealing with countries and businesses that want to remain on the cutting edge, there is going to be a lot of competition, and they are going to do everything they possibly can to ensure that that takes place.

Ambassador Hills is absolutely right, the imperative of focusing on the rights of property is a very, very important thing, and I will say she and I were just discussing earlier today that as nations become more innovative and creative, and as they develop patents themselves, and we were talking about the fact that in China, we are seeing a dramatic increase in the number of patents being created. As that kind of intellectual property is developed there, you are going to see a greater degree of responsibility take place.

Mr. SALMON. It seems like, I mean, in a nutshell, what is happening is, and I have heard it probably more associated with some of our pharmaceutical companies that go over there, and the generic companies appeal the process, saying that they haven't really lived up to everything they promised to deliver, and so the patents should be invalidated and they should be able to go ahead and come in and take over those patents in the generic form.

As I have talked to some of my friends from Canada, they say, well, that is going through the courts. But I think there are two opportunities maybe that we are going to have to look at. One is I think Canada could address it through their legislative process, to make sure that that is clarified and that IPR protection is paramount to them as it is to us; and, then, secondly, there is always the possibility of, we hate to do it, but filing a claim. I don't want to rule that out.

One last question, and that is dealing with energy. I am as excited as I can be to see what is happening in Mexico right now and them making the constitutional changes to allow investment from foreign oil companies and foreign partners, and I think it is going to do dramatic things to provide energy for the entire continent.

But one of the things that kind of seems stymied still is the XL pipeline, and I know that our friends from Canada are very, very concerned about the length of time where we have been dragging our feet. Any thoughts from either of you on, you know, what we should do to move forward on that, the XL pipeline itself?

Mr. DREIER. Well, I am on record when I served here. Clearly, I am very supportive of proceeding with the XL pipeline, and for all the reasons that have been stated, to me it is very obvious and apparent. And I think it is also something that can help us in our relationship with Canada.

As you know, Mr. Chairman, next month, Prime Minister Harper will be meeting with Presidents Obama and Peña Nieto, and I think that this will clearly be a topic of discussion, I suspect, and I also want to say that as we look at this overall issue, I want to congratulate Secretary Kerry for the very strong speech that he delivered at the Organization of American States recently in which he talked about this expansion of our trade relationship within this hemisphere. I think it is an important and a very positive sign of this administration's desire to move forward on it, and I hope that the XL pipeline will be part of that process.

Mr. SALMON. Thank you.

The chair recognizes Mr. Sires.

Mr. SIRES. Thank you, Mr. Chairman.

You know, intellectual property is one of the big issues for me. Obviously, coming from a pharmaceutical State like New Jersey, you know, we consider ourselves the medicine capital of America, so many jobs.

But it seems like the barrier in Canada is just one. We seem to get—China hacks into our computers, tries to steal our property. Russia does the same thing, all these other countries. It seems that our companies here in this country are bombarded with people trying to steal our research.

And then you come to a friend, which I consider Canada to be, and then we have this barrier, which seems very silly, on pharmaceuticals when it has been proven already to be useful and they come up with generics. I don't know if the courts are ever going to solve this. I think we have to take, I don't know, firmer steps to get them moving in the direction where they can set some standards so we can really put this beside us and go on to the next issue because one of the issues that I have with the South Korean trade agreement was the intellectual properties, you know, of our companies.

So I was just wondering with NAFTA, what are some of the things that we could improve on that maybe we didn't look at in terms of intellectual property and other factors? What did we miss in this?

Mr. DREIER. Let me, before Ambassador Hills, let me just defend her a little bit and let's look at the time frame of this. We are marking the 20th anniversary. Think about where we as a world were 20 years ago. Where was the Internet 20 years ago? I read Eric Farnsworth's testimony. He underscores that in his remarks. It was virtually nonexistent.

Now, obviously the pharmaceutical industry existed, but the kinds of advances that have been made in the last two decades have been monumental as well, and I think that it is important to note, to say that things were missed or there were mistakes that were made, most of this has been what has taken place in the two decades that have followed the passage and implementation of the North American Free Trade Agreement.

And I think one of the important things that needs to be done as we look at negotiations for the future, and I have argued this for the Trans-Pacific Partnership, is to have a degree of fluidity and flexibility so that as other countries are able to meet certain guidelines and standards, that they can become part of these agreements as well, and so I think that one of the important things that needs to be done is not be too rigid within the structure. So I just say that partially in defense of Ambassador Hills.

Mr. SIRES. You know, when I say that I mean because I want it to move forward and be better.

Mr. DREIER. Right. Absolutely.

Mr. SIRES. You know, I don't want it to just——

Mr. DREIER. Right.

Ambassador HILLS. Well, let me say that the agreement at the time provided the highest level of patent, trademark, copyright, trade secret protection that had been negotiated anywhere, and as David Dreier has just stated, a lot of change has taken place. So we can enhance those rules through the mechanism of the Trans-Pacific Partnership, for example, we have got three mega agreements that we could address and strengthen the rules, but why not sit down at the leaders meeting with Canada and talk about how this erodes the partnership?

And I do believe that our northern and southern neighbors would like to join, for example, the Transatlantic agreement, but if we have differences that create friction, it will be difficult to pull that off, and so talking about it, working your way through it, and trying to get the rules to cover good intellectual property of pharmaceuticals, which is primarily the problem in Canada, I think it can be done, but it can't be ignored.

Mr. DREIER. Let me just add, if I could, that I think that Ambassador Hills raises a very important point, and that is, my personal view as we look at TTIP, the Transatlantic Trade Investment Partnership, that the idea of doing a U.S.-European Union free trade agreement is a nice start, but by virtue of the fact that we have had so much success with the North American Free Trade Agreement, I am one who believes that the idea of making this a NAFTA–EU free trade agreement would actually be much more beneficial to both our country and to the hemisphere and the global economy as well, and so I would hope very much that we would have the chance to move forward in that area.

Ambassador HILLS. I fully agree with this. I think we actually will diminish our gains if we don't do that, and that is because we are unique in North America. As I said, we not only sell things to one another, we make things together, and our markets are so interlinked that 40 cents of every product that we import is U.S. content.

If we have different rules of origin with Europe, this simply won't work. It will destroy the NAFTA platform that has given us so much and the statistics that the chairman mentioned about the gains that we have already achieved. So this is an imperative that I hope Congress takes a good hard look at it.

Mr. SIRES. Well, I don't want to beat up on Canada too much, but the chairman and I are working on a bill to extend the amount of time Canadians can stay in this country from 6 to 8 months. So we will work on that.

Mr. SALMON. Thank you.

The chair recognizes Mr. Radel.

Mr. RADEL. Thank you, Mr. Chair.

Regardless of some of the positions I have found my own self in life, I have always been the eternal optimist, and as we look at NAFTA and some of the very real effects that it has had on people and their jobs, there have been incredibly positive things that have come, big picture things that both Democrats and Republicans cannot deny and can agree on to move forward. National security, just an easy one. When you have got a good working relationship with people, you are going to have a solid relationship to move forward and not have any stresses or strenuous relationship moving forward.

The other issue here, too, as we talk about countries, even more specifically south of us, is the hot topic of immigration. No one can deny, one of the best ways to solve an illegal immigration problem in the United States is to make sure men and women coming from other countries can put food on their kids' plate, and the best way to do that is to be able to provide economic security, jobs, and that is exactly what we have been able to do for years with this, and I commend you both for your work on this.

Just some general questions. What more can we, what more can the Federal Government cap do to help facilitate shared manufacturing production?

Ambassador, you put it right. We make things together. What more can we do to provide more of that certainty and stability to keep this and to move forward in more free trade around the world?

Ambassador HILLS. It has already been mentioned that the infrastructure going north and south is poor, and sometimes a truck bringing that component part that we need to be globally competitive is held up at the border, not for just an hour but sometimes many hours. And they come to the border, and as you know, they have to unload, get a lorry, take it across the border, put it on, so it has three trucks in effect that have to carry this component that our manufacturers are waiting for.

This is a cost in terms of time. This is a cost in terms of money, and that makes us less competitive for those markets that don't have that extra cost. Because of Mexico and Canada's proximity to us, that makes us more competitive so that when lower cost countries in Asia, for example, seek to compete, they have a transportation cost. We are adding a transportation complexity cost that could be avoided. So we ought to give some thought to that, have a real plan for how we address it.

We perhaps, at least in my view, have been remiss on how we have handled the trucking issue with Mexico, and if we expect other nations to adhere to agreements, then, of course, we must, too.

Mr. DREIER. Let me just add to that. Thank you, Mr. Radel.

The Economist had an interesting piece on NAFTA 20 in which they pointed, as we all do, with great regularity at September 11th of 2001. Very, very sadly what happened on September 11th played a big role in undermining the ability to deal with the immigration issue. It exacerbated the tension at our borders, and I think that, obviously, border security is critically important, and it is something that needs to be addressed. And I always argued when I was privileged to serve in this House that the number one responsibility of the Federal Government is our Nation's security. So we can't forget that.

We also know that with these agreements, it is important for us to realize the fact that infrastructure has to be improved. I was very concerned about the trucking issue, as Ambassador Hills has said, and I think that we need to do everything that we can to make it as easy as possible for this free flow of goods, services, capital, information, ideas, and people to take place. We have so many opportunities to work together.

We all in our freshman economics class in college learned the economic theory of comparative advantage. Comparative advantage says we do what we do best, and The Economist underscored the bombardier Learjet example of Pratt and Whitney designing the aircraft here, the assembling taking place in Wichita, and in Quertaro, Mexico, we saw manufacturing take place obviously at a company that is now owned by Canada.

The only thing done outside of this hemisphere is done in Ireland, and that is the wing manufacture. The market itself is going to play a role in determining what Canada, the United States, and Mexico will do, and I have a great deal of confidence in it.

Mr. RADEL. I agree 100 percent.

With my time winding down, I would just once again thank you both so much.

And thank you, Mr. Chair, for calling this.

Mr. SALMON. Thank you.

The chair recognizes Mr. Meeks.

Mr. MEEKS. Thank you, Mr. Chairman.

I enjoyed listening to you and couldn't agree more on many of the points that you have raised. You know, as we enter into negotiations for TPA, which we have to figure out in a bipartisan way to pass, and then dealing with TPP and TTIP, all very important.

Oftentimes, I ask, you know, we see other nations are entering into trade agreements, and I think as the Ambassador indicated, we need to get in the game and negotiate and have our own trade agreements or be a part of it like TPP, which I think would elevate standards, our standards, because if we stay on the sideline and let them negotiate with China, for example, or others, then you could expect that those standards will be lower and not the high standards that we set in our trade agreements.

So I think it becomes tremendously important for us. Basically, and I think it is exactly what Mr. Dreier has indicated, the fact that 20 years ago so much has changed, there has been so much— the economy and technology is so different today than it was 20 years ago, and the world is so much smaller today than it was 20 years ago, it becomes that much more important for us to engage.

That being said, we have got to figure out here how to make sure that we do it in a bipartisan way and understand that, actually, when you look at most of the trade agreements, it changes our trade deficit. Our trade deficit goes down because markets that had not been open to us, where we could not sell our goods that were made in America, now are open so that we can sell those goods to those individuals. That is where in fact the majority of the buyers are. So if we are going to expand, it has to be outside of the borders of the United States of America. And that is why that is so important.

So all that to say now, in trying to do a bipartisan deal and trying to work collectively together, there was a ground—what I believe was a groundbreaking trade compromise known as the May 10th agreement in which we—there was significant update and change for I believe the better, a better way that we negotiate trade pacts.

So my first question to you, do you think that the May 10th deal addresses many of the concerns that some, rightly or wrongly, you know, when people talked about NAFTA because you still hear NAFTA as if it was something that was drafted yesterday and not something that you could build upon, but do you think that it addressed some of those concerns?

And how can we build upon that, which I think that will help us go into the direction of this shouldn't be an issue, this shouldn't be a Democrat or Republican issue. This is an issue that is important for the United States whether you are Democrat or Republican.

Ambassador HILLS. I agree with you that trade is absolutely vital.

If you look at what is the fuel for our economic growth today, trade is essential, and the trade promotion authority is extremely important. It is not only important because of the division in our Government where you have power over trade and finance, but the President has negotiating power.

Our trading partners don't want to sit at the table with us and put their tough political issues on the table unless they know that the agreement is fairly going to be voted up or down. If the agreement is not a good one, vote it down, but if the agreement is one that you think is good, don't unravel it with amendments that are going to destroy the agreement, and the prospect of that means that you don't get as high a quality of agreement as you otherwise would get.

But how do we deal with the changes? Yes, globalization has absolutely transformed the world. I mean, I suspect that you didn't use a computer in 1989. There are so many things that we didn't do and didn't have 20 years ago.

How do we build on the NAFTA? Well, we have a wonderful opportunity with, for example, the Trans-Pacific Partnership. We don't have to reopen NAFTA. Our two neighbors are sitting at the table with us. And whatever we agree to in the Trans-Pacific Partnership that changes, upgrades, adds to the NAFTA will be the governing document.

So we really want to get on with this and get a really good Asia-Pacific agreement. And my hope is that we can achieve the promise that we made that we would have an agreement that covered all of Asia-Pacific, all of APEC, all the 21 economies. But this is a first step, and we should make it a good one.

Mr. DREIER. And I suspect that the May 10th concerns that were raised will clearly be part of the TPP negotiating process. And that will, as the Ambassador has said, be the vehicle that will allow many of these concerns that Mr. Sires and that others have raised to effectively be dealt with.

Mr. MEEKS. I am out of time, I know, but if I had time, I would ask you about Trade Adjustment Assistance and whether you think that would fall in. I think it is important because some—we have lost, I believe, more jobs because of technological advances than we have because of trade. But I am out of time, and so I will leave that for another time.

Mr. DREIER. It has expired, but I will say that I do believe that, as we proceed in a bipartisan way, that Trade Adjustment Assistance will continue to need to be part of the process itself.

Ambassador HILLS. And I think it is actually helpful, because we know that trade creates growth generally, but there are some dislocations. And for our Nation, it is very good to have Trade Adjustment Assistance.

Mr. SALMON. Thank you.

The chair recognizes Mr. Duncan.

Mr. DUNCAN. Thank you, Mr. Chairman.

And, Mr. Dreier, welcome back to Congress.

Mr. DREIER. Thank you very much.

Mr. DUNCAN. You are missed, your leadership is missed, your composure in difficult issues is missed. And you were a role model for a lot of us to follow in how you handled yourself as a Congressman. So, again, I say welcome back.

There are a lot of issues with trade. I met with the members of Parliament that are part of a transatlantic group on terrorism last year, and we discussed TTIP. And they were very interested in seeing that trade agreement move forward at some point.

They raised some concerns about agricultural products from the U.S. and Europe. I think that is a challenge that we are going to have to address. If you want to touch on that, we will get to that in a second.

And then I would like to talk about energy, primarily. This may be for Mr. Farnsworth more than this panel. But with what Mexico is seeing with their energy sector, with the denationalization of the energy sector and Pemex and more competitiveness down there in future years, how do you think the NAFTA countries will benefit from more energy resources here in North America? And how does that apply to trade?

And then the last thing I will mention is with TPP. And I have to support the textile industry in South Carolina. What we saw with the Korean Free Trade Agreement, the reason I voted against it was the fact it felt likes textiles were sort of thrown to the wolves there at the end of the negotiations at the end of the Bush administration and were treated unfairly with Korea. So we are very cognizant of what is going on with Vietnam and with dumping and countries of origin with regard to textiles.

And then the last thing I would touch on is, we need to make sure that, with MTBs, we have companies like Michelin and Bridgestone that have certain raw materials that are vital to the production of tires in South Carolina, and a lot of times they have to get a miscellaneous tariff benefit changed in order to get those raw materials in so that those jobs can be kept in South Carolina and not sent to Brazil or Asia, where the resources may be a little more plentiful.

So those three things: Energy primarily, the textile issue, MTBs, and also agricultural products. If you all just want to touch on those, and I will just open it up for you.

Ambassador?

Ambassador HILLS. Well, we certainly should address the agricultural issues. We have 90 percent of our subsidies going to five commodities: Corn, wheat, soy, cotton, and rice. And if nothing goes to string beans or apples—and you hear about all the health foods in the world, but with our economy in the financial state it is in and the commodity prices being relatively generous, it would be very well that we would be able to address this issue. And Europe, for the same reason, it could move on these issues.

That ability to talk about agriculture would get us services put by other countries on the table, where we have tremendous competitive advantage. But if you have nothing to put on the table, you are going to get nothing given to you on the table.

And so agriculture is absolutely key. When I said we have relatively low tariffs with Europe on products, agriculture is the exception. Agriculture, textiles, glassware, footwear, you take those out and our average tariffs is about 3 percent. You put those things in and you have dislocations.

And as far as energy goes, you know, inviting Mexico in the TTIP would provide President Peña an umbrella to talk about a major trade agreement that would help him move forward on his economic reforms that we want him to make. He has put through the energy constitution. He still has to get legislation, he still has to have regulation. We want him to move forward and liberalize telecommunications. If he were part of the team negotiating to make North America more competitive, it would make all the difference in the world.

And that is what Salinas did with the NAFTA. He used that as an umbrella and said, well, folks, look at what I am getting, so please stay with me; I want this trade agreement, and you will get something for it. I think that this should be part of our strategic thinking.

Mr. DREIER. Let me just add, I don't have an opinion on the MTB issue as it relates to those. But I will tell you that, Mr. Duncan, I feel very strongly about the so-called Pacto, which is the reform that President Peña Nieto has boldly pursued. And he is working, and it has been challenging to bring together the three major political parties in Mexico. But the idea of dealing not only with telecommunications and energy but labor and education and fiscal reform, those five areas, is something that is really groundbreaking.

I mean, you know, we have talked about the fact that I, you know, hung around this place for more than a couple of years. And if you go back to the 1980s—and you guys are too young to remember that, but I will tell you that I remember very vividly. It is when I started here. And I was younger than you when I started here doing that. But I will say that, at that time, the struggles that existed between our two countries were very, very great. And the idea of looking at political reform, the five things that I just mentioned within the Pacto, the fact that—the Woodrow Wilson study the other day pointed to the fact that, going back to the 1980s, the average Mexican family lived in a one-room home; today they live in three-room homes. I mean, there are so many advances that have been made.

And I believe that that is going to enure to the benefit of your constituents in South Carolina. Why? Because as we see that economy growing—Mr. Sires pointed out correctly, we still have very serious poverty problems that exist in Mexico and the United States. The displacement Ambassador Hills correctly pointed to is why we need Trade Adjustment Assistance. But I believe that as we see these economies grow, they are going to provide a market— they are going to provide a market for the workers you have in your congressional district. And I think that is something that needs to be remembered.

It is not going to be perfect, and it is not going to remain exactly as it is. But, I mean, we believe in the marketplace itself. And, you know, Ronald Reagan really envisaged this on November 6th of 1979 when he announced his candidacy for President. 1979, Ronald Reagan, in that announcement, said that he envisaged an accord of trade among all the Americas. This was part of the Reagan vision that was then implemented by the Bush-Hills team and then passed through the Congress by the Clinton-Kantor team.

And I will say that I think this is going to be a real winner for your constituents as we move ahead with it.

Mr. DUNCAN. Thank you for that. And I appreciate the testimony.

I yield back.

Mr. SALMON. Thank you very much.

That concludes the questions. We would love to thank our distinguished first panel.

Mr. DREIER. Thanks very much. It was a great honor to be able to be back and see you guys.

Ambassador HILLS. Great pleasure to join you.

Mr. SALMON. Thank you very much.

I would like to change the panels now and have the second panel be seated.

We might let the second panel know, we have been notified that our vote on the omnibus budget, or appropriations bill, excuse me, is going to take place. It was supposed to be sometime in the last 15 minutes. So if it buzzes and we have to leave, please be patient. We will be back. It is the last vote of the day, and quite an important one.

So, with that, we will go ahead and dispense with introductions just to save time. I ask for unanimous consent to go ahead and do that. Without objection, and we will go ahead and start with you, Mr. Farnsworth.

### STATEMENT OF MR. ERIC FARNSWORTH, VICE PRESIDENT, COUNCIL OF THE AMERICAS AND AMERICAS SOCIETY

Mr. FARNSWORTH. Well, thank you very much, Mr. Chairman. Good afternoon to you, to the members of the subcommittee, Mr. Sires. It is a real honor to have the opportunity to appear before you again this afternoon.

And I do want to reemphasize the fact that this is a continuation, as well, of the field hearing from Tucson, which was a real success. And it is a particular pleasure, as well, to join other witnesses today of such prominence and stature.

If I may, let me give you what I believe to be the bottom line first: NAFTA was first and foremost an agreement designed to increase trade and investment among its three parties, promote North American economic integration, and support a vision of open market democracy for Mexico, providing that Nation with a clear path toward political and economic modernization.

On all three priorities, NAFTA has succeeded. As we have already heard, since 1993 U.S. trade in goods and services with Canada and Mexico has increased from $370 billion a year to over $1 trillion today. Annual trade between the United States and Canada has more than doubled; with Mexico, it has more than quadrupled. More than 40 U.S. States count either Mexico or Canada as their top export destination.

Perhaps more importantly even than those statistics, however, NAFTA institutionalized a vision for North America that would have been impossible absent significant political and economic reforms in Mexico, and NAFTA both catalyzed such reforms and has also benefited from them.

Trade agreements are not just about trade and investment. They are also critical, if often overlooked, tools of U.S. foreign policy. Unquestionably, NAFTA has directly supported Mexico's democratic transformation over the past 20 years, thus contributing to the true partnership that now exists between our two countries. In fact, we are allies in a way that 20 years ago it was almost inconceivable to even consider.

It has empowered new constituencies in Mexico and a growing middle class that has demanded and received an increasingly clear political voice. And as we see Mexico's economy generate new opportunities, coupled with the slowdown of the U.S. economy, net migration flows from Mexico have become virtually zero, reducing the temperature on this bilateral irritant. A full accounting of

NAFTA's impact, therefore, cannot overlook these very important issues.

Since NAFTA was implemented, however, the world has changed dramatically. As a result, the agreement should be modernized, I believe, to expand North American competitiveness. Three trends show why.

First, production models have changed, and we have already heard a little bit about that this afternoon. Our three countries don't just trade products together, we now design and make these products together. And that is to our benefit. The statistic has already been used; let me use it again. Every dollar from U.S. imports from Mexico includes some 40 percent of U.S. content; from Canada, it is some 25 percent. So North America is now the production platform.

Second, in 1994, there was barely an Internet, as Mr. Dreier said. Nobody had a clue how radically electronic communications would fundamentally alter business models. More broadly, incredible technological advances have transformed virtually every sector in the past 2 decades, from energy, which we have heard about, to health care, which we have heard about, to financial services. The list goes on and on. Industries that were not even contemplated by original negotiators are now significant engines of growth.

Third, there is a noticeable change in trade patterns within North America demarcated by 9/11, at which point the border thickened and commercial activities understandably took a second seat to security. Still, as NAFTA-facilitated trade has increased, infrastructure has generally languished.

Our strategic opportunity, therefore, is to capitalize on our increasingly unified North American economic space and dynamism, particularly as Mexico advances along its reform agenda. An agenda for progress that we might consider, then, would include several elements, in some areas addressing challenges stemming from the original agreement, and in others taking note of changes in the North American production model and finding ways to facilitate and enhance such activities.

As a first step, we need to find a way to get the greatest efficiencies from the agreement as it currently exists, from trucking regulations to intellectual property protections, to customs and regulatory harmonization, to border infrastructure. These are not easy issues. Some have been with us since the agreement was concluded. Some require additional funding.

At the same time, were the original agreement to be negotiated today, it likely would not look the same. For example, it would have to incorporate the incredible advances in energy that are making North America self-sufficient, improving our terms of trade, while igniting a manufacturing reconnaissance. It would highlight and promote the rapid growth in services in newer industries, like biotech, that has occurred in the past generation, including the information technology revolution and cloud computing. It might incorporate some categories of labor mobility. It would seek ways to safely increase border throughput as a strategic economic issue for the entire United States, not just border States. And it would attempt to find effective ways to address rule-of-law issues, as former President Zedillo has written recently, or perhaps Mexico's most vexing challenge. We have talked a little bit about Canada; it also applies to Mexico.

More broadly, the NAFTA bloc should be viewed as the basis for a more strategic trade policy generally. Mexican and Canadian entry into TPP was critical, and we have talked about that already. Now, to take advantage of economies of scale, we should also negotiate, together with Mexico and Canada, the free-trade agreement with the European Union. And, similarly—and I don't think we have talked about this quite yet today—an early economic association among North American and Pacific Alliance nations, which include Mexico, Colombia, Peru, and Chile, would be both timely and appropriate.

The upcoming leaders' meeting that we have talked about in Mexico will offer an opportunity to take stock of North America and to begin a process that builds on NAFTA while even updating it further. The leaders should commit to annual trilateral meetings, designating a senior official to promote progress in the interim. They should commit to a process that includes the private sector, whereby the unrealized gains from NAFTA can be identified and addressed and those lessons learned from the agreement can be directly applied elsewhere. And they should begin a dialogue with the leaders of the Pacific Alliance and other nations in the hemisphere that will advance discussions on hemispheric economic integration, even as the Summit of the Americas has lost its primary economic focus.

Given changed circumstances both within North America and outside the region in larger emerging markets, such as China and India and others, it is time to have another look to determine where further progress can be made.

Mr. Chairman, I really want to thank you again for this opportunity. I have appreciated it. I look forward to your questions. Mr. Sires, thank you very much.

Mr. SALMON. Thank you, Mr. Farnsworth.

[The prepared statement of Mr. Farnsworth follows:]

## NAFTA AT TWENTY: ACCOMPLISHMENTS, CHALLENGES, AND THE WAY FORWARD

HEARING BEFORE THE U.S. HOUSE OF REPRESENTATIVES
COMMITTEE ON FOREIGN AFFAIRS
SUBCOMMITTEE ON THE WESTERN HEMISPHERE
JANUARY 15, 2013

ERIC FARNSWORTH
VICE PRESIDENT
COUNCIL OF THE AMERICAS

\*\*\* As Prepared for Delivery \*\*\*

Good afternoon, Mr. Chairman and Members. Thank you for the opportunity to testify before you on such a timely and important topic. This hearing today continues your outstanding efforts to help build a better North America, and I congratulate and thank you for your ongoing leadership. It is a true honor to appear before you this afternoon, continuing from your important field hearing in Tucson late last year, and a particular pleasure to join other witnesses of such prominence and stature.

The Council of the Americas is a Long-Term Champion for North America

As you know, the Council of the Americas has a history of engagement in promoting a more economically integrated North America. From the time of our founding we organized and ran the U.S. section of the Mexico-U.S. Business Council (MEXUS), which was instrumental in advocating for the idea and passage of a North American Free Trade Agreement (NAFTA). After working for several years on NAFTA implementation issues, MEXUS was re-organized into the North American Business Committee. The Council also served as the co-secretariat for the United States of the North American Competitiveness Council, a group of business leaders from Canada, Mexico, and the United States formed in 2006 and active until 2009. The NACC coordinated advice from the private sector to present to the three North American leaders primarily on ways to enhance North America's competitive position.

In 2012, we established the North American Border and Competitiveness Leadership Initiative, a public-private dialogue on reducing constraints on intra-regional trade. Most recently, the Council has also been very active in the context of the U.S.-Mexico High-Level Economic Dialogue launched in September with Vice President Biden in Mexico. We continue to lead an effort to provide private sector input to U.S. and Mexican cabinet officials on actionable ideas for the two governments to improve binational economic growth and development. And we look forward to the North American foreign ministers meeting here in Washington later this week, and the next meeting of the North American leaders next month in Toluca, Mexico.

Council of the Americas
1615 L Street, NW
Suite 250
Washington, DC 20036
www.as-coa.org

This year, 2014, is an important one for trade, and NAFTA plays an important role. Our efforts to build the US trade agenda will prove to be more successful and strategic to the extent that the United States and our trading partners have a solid understanding of the accomplishments and challenges of NAFTA and the way forward. And in my view, along with the Panama Canal whose 100 year anniversary we celebrate this year, NAFTA is one of the two most important experiments in hemispheric trade and economic growth.

## NAFTA Has Been a Success both in Economic and Foreign Policy

Mr. Chairman and Members of the Subcommittee, let me give you the bottom line first: NAFTA was a true innovation in economic relations. It was first and foremost an agreement designed to increase trade and investment among its three parties; promote North American economic integration; and support a vision of open market democracy for Mexico providing that nation with a clear path toward political and economic modernization. On all three metrics, NAFTA has succeeded.

Since 1993, U.S. trade in goods and services with Canada and Mexico increased from $307 billion to over $1 *trillion* by 2012. Annual trade between the United States and Canada has more than doubled; with Mexico trade has quadrupled. Canada is the top trading partner of the United States and Mexico is our second largest export market and third largest trading partner. More than 40 states count either Canada or Mexico as their top export destination. Perhaps more importantly, beyond these tangible commercial benefits, NAFTA institutionalized a vision for North America that would have been impossible absent significant political and economic reforms in Mexico, both catalyzing such reforms and also benefitting from them.

This is one reason why we are so pleased that this hearing today is being held by this Subcommittee. Fundamentally, trade agreements like NAFTA are not just about trade and investment, they are also critical if often overlooked tools of U.S. foreign policy. On the basis of economic growth, jobs created, and other common indicators, NAFTA has been a success, even if it has not perhaps been the panacea for all ills that proponents of the agreement sometimes seemed to be suggesting that it would be in order to pass and implement the agreement. Inversely, neither has NAFTA been responsible for all the ills that are frequently attributed to it by opponents.

Unquestionably, however, NAFTA has directly supported Mexico's democratic transformation over the past 20 years by requiring legislative and regulatory changes that might not otherwise have occurred absent an external catalyst. It has also empowered new economic constituencies and a growing middle class that has demanded and received an increasingly clear political voice. Arguably, Mexico's politics are more transparent and democratic today than ever before, and the Mexican people have made clear their disinterest in returning to the ways of the past. And as we see Mexico's economy generate and offer new opportunities to its workers, coupled with the slowdown of the U.S. economy since 2008, net migration flows from Mexico have become virtually zero. A full accounting of NAFTA's impact cannot overlook these issues.

From the trade perspective, NAFTA was at the cutting edge when it was passed originally. Heretofore there had never been an effort to link the world's largest, most developed economy with an economically backward, underdeveloped neighbor that seemed to lurch from economic crisis to crisis. The gulf between Mexico and its two other North American neighbors was large and perhaps insurmountable. At the same time, the pre-existing free trade agreement that the United States had already implemented with Canada was cause for Ottawa to join the talks as a defensive move, so as not to see their own benefits eroded by a U.S. agreement with Mexico. Along with certain constitutional and political restrictions in all three countries, this meant that negotiators could move ahead only so far, excluding certain sectors such as energy or labor mobility because they were too politically controversial at the time. What the negotiators created, however, proved to be an effective framework for ordering the majority of North American trade and investment relations during the economic stresses, political transitions, and security crises of the past 20 years.

<u>But the World has Changed in the Past 20 Years, and NAFTA has Become Dated</u>

Since then, however, the world has changed dramatically, and NAFTA is now showing its age. It should therefore be modernized as a means to promote a joint vision of true North American competitiveness. Otherwise, NAFTA could potentially become an agreement that actually sets a virtual limit on North American trade relations rather than a powerful tool to unlock them to their fullest potential.

Three trends must be highlighted.

First, production models have changed. Canada, Mexico, and the United States do not merely trade products; we now design and make them together. In many industries, joint production and supply chains have developed to such an extent that, from the commercial perspective at least, national borders no longer define products. This is to our benefit: according to the National Bureau of Economic Statistics, every dollar of U.S. imports from Mexico, for example, includes some 40 percent of U.S. content; for Canada it is 25 percent. As a result it is no longer accurate to think in terms of U.S. or Mexican or Canadian products when North America itself has become the production platform. North America has become a true 21$^{st}$ century economic space, just in time to compete more effectively with China, India, and others.

Second, consider that in 1994, there was barely an internet, much less Facebook or Twitter (incidentally, follow me on @ericfarns...). One of the first emails I remember receiving, in fact, was actually from Carla Hills in 1992 when she was the US Trade Representative and I was a junior member of the NAFTA negotiation team; email itself was very new and nobody had a clue how radically and rapidly electronic communications would fundamentally alter business models around the world. But it's not just email and social media. Consider the incredible advances that technology has made possible in the auto and manufacturing sectors, energy, financial services, IT, medical products, agriculture, and virtually every other economic sector in the past two decades. Entire industries that were not even contemplated by NAFTA are now a significant part of all three economies. Yet, while there is a process to make technical fixes to NAFTA and that process continues to be utilized, the fact remains that the agreement is a 20th century trade platform undergirding our 21st century economies.

Third, there is a noticeable change in trade patterns within North America demarcated by 9/11, at which point the border "thickened" and commercial activities understandably took a second seat to security. A resulting lack of attention to commercial needs at the borders, specifically in cross-border infrastructure but in other areas too, has created unnecessary bottlenecks and wait times for commercial traffic that erode the compelling advantages of geographic proximity. As NAFTA-facilitated trade has increased, infrastructure has generally languished. In fact, the last border crossing established between the United States and Mexico was over 100 years ago. That means that our 21st century economies, undergirded by a 20th century trade framework, are utilizing 19th century infrastructure.

As trade increases, this picture will continue to get worse.

Moving Toward the Future

Our strategic opportunity, therefore, is to capitalize on our increasingly unified North American economic space and dynamism, particularly as Mexico advances concretely along its reform agenda. In this 20th year of NAFTA, the moment is ripe to think bigger and bolder about North America and regional competitiveness. If we do so, viewing North America as a more unified production platform and our borders as lines that unite rather than divide our three great nations, the way forward will become increasingly clear.

And in that regard, a path forward would include several important elements, in some areas attempting to improve challenges stemming from the original agreement, and in others taking note of changes in the North American production model and working to find ways to facilitate and enhance such activities.

As a first step we really do need to find a way to get the greatest efficiencies from the agreement as it currently exists, from trucking regulations to intellectual property protections to customs and regulatory harmonization to border infrastructure. These are not easy issues; some have been with us since the agreement was concluded, some require additional funding. The meeting of North American leaders next month would present a powerful opportunity to recommit all three governments to addressing them.

At the same time, were the original agreement to be negotiated today it likely would not look the same. For example, it would have to incorporate the incredible advances in energy that are making North America self-sufficient, improving terms of trade while igniting a manufacturing renaissance with lower cost energy supplies. It would highlight and promote the rapid growth in services that has occurred in the past generation, including the information technology revolution and cloud computing. It might incorporate some categories of labor mobility (and without doubt U.S. immigration reform independent of any trade agreement would directly contribute to economic well-being). It would seek ways to minimize the existing sand-in-the-gears of border commerce, looking for ways to safely increase border throughput as a strategic economic issue for the entire United States, not just border states. It would attempt to find effective ways to improve the rule of law, which remains Mexico's most vexing challenge according to former president Ernesto Zedillo in the forthcoming Americas Quarterly.

More broadly, the NAFTA bloc should be viewed as the basis for a more strategic trade policy generally. Mexican and Canadian entry into the Trans-Pacific Partnership negotiations—which the Council began to promote immediately after the United States announced its intent to join the negotiations—was a critical step. Now, to take full advantage of economies of scale, we should also consider negotiating together with Mexico and Canada the free trade agreement with the European Union. Similarly, an early economic association among the NAFTA and Pacific Alliance nations including Chile, Colombia, and Peru in addition to Mexico would be both timely and appropriate.

The meeting of North American leaders next month in Mexico will offer a tremendous opportunity to take stock of the NAFTA agreement to date, and to begin a process that builds on NAFTA even while updating it further. The leaders should commit at a minimum to annual trilateral meetings, which will drive the agenda and keep these issues at the forefront, and allow for greater coordination to the extent appropriate for the broader trade agenda. They should commit to a process that includes the private sector whereby the unrealized gains from NAFTA can be identified and addressed, and lessons learned from the agreement can be directly applied to the TPP and TTIP negotiations. And they should begin a dialogue with the leaders of the Pacific Alliance and other nations that will advance discussions on hemispheric economic integration even as the Summit of the Americas, which was originally conceived as the primary forum for region wide economic discussions, has lost its primary economic focus.

No negotiation ever produces a perfect result, especially when the issues under negotiation are at the vanguard of what's been done before. So it was with NAFTA 20 years ago, but the results have nonetheless proven the test of time. Now, given changed circumstances both within North America and also outside the region in the larger emerging markets such as China, India, and others, it's time to have another look to determine where further progress can be made.

Thank you, again, Mr. Chairman, for the opportunity to be with you today, and I look forward to your questions.

Mr. SALMON. Mr. Elliot.

## STATEMENT OF MR. MARK T. ELLIOT, EXECUTIVE VICE PRESIDENT, GLOBAL INTELLECTUAL PROPERTY CENTER, U.S. CHAMBER OF COMMERCE

Mr. ELLIOT. Thank you, Chairman Salmon and Ranking Member Sires. The U.S. Chamber of Commerce appreciates your leadership and the opportunity to testify on IP matters associated with NAFTA today.

From the outset, I would like to state that the NAFTA has succeeded spectacularly in boosting cross-border trade, economic growth, and creating good jobs. It has proven to be one of the most effective and beneficial trade agreements in U.S. history. As we celebrate the triumph of NAFTA on its 20th anniversary, the U.S. Chamber of Commerce calls upon elected officials and business leaders in Canada, Mexico, and the United States to build upon this foundation in the years ahead.

One area where particular focus is needed is that of intellectual property. At the time of signing, NAFTA included IP language that was of a high standard. However, since the agreement was signed, 20 years has passed, and this level of intellectual property protection now represents a very low bar by 2014 standards.

In the past 2 years, we have highlighted industry concerns with the Canadian and Mexican IP environments through the USTR Special 301 process. In 2012, the U.S. Chamber of Commerce released an international IP index, which was the first-ever comprehensive review of national IP environments, covering 11 key markets. The United States and the United Kingdom and Australia all performed well in this regard. On the other hand, Mexico and Canada were more closely linked to Russia, Malaysia, and China.

In Mexico, we have seen some forward progression in recent years. The business community has been working well with the Mexican Government. In contrast, Canada's relatively low score results in wide-ranging IP problems and a distinct lack of action from the Canadian Government. It is fair to say that industry is more concerned with the IP environment in Canada than in Mexico. And I would like to provide a few specific examples of some of the Canadian issues.

Firstly, WTO TRIPS and NAFTA require patents to be granted for inventions that are new, non-obvious, and useful. This is also known as patent utility. Over the past 8 years, the Canadian courts have used this clause to revoke more than 20 pharmaceutical patents for what they call "lack of utility or usefulness." They have justified doing so by requiring evidence that is wholly inappropriate for judicial review or patent approvals. In one instance, an innovative pharmaceutical company lost $500 million in revenue. This trend is not happening anywhere else in the world.

Secondly, and unlike other countries, Canada has yet to provide ex officio authority to its customs officials to seize counterfeit and pirated products at the border.

Thirdly, the business community is concerned with the ongoing and substantial illicit trafficking of goods across the U.S.-Canadian border. Counterfeiting and piracy in Canada are worth approximately $20 billion to $30 billion annually. This includes sporting goods, medicines, consumer electronics, automotive parts. The list is endless. Many of these counterfeits originate from China, and the criminal organizations see Canada as the easiest entry point into North America.

Fourthly, if a pharmaceutical patent is successfully challenged by a generic manufacturer, the patent holder has no administrative right of appeal. However, if the patent holder is successful in defending the patent, the generic manufacturer is entitled to administrative appeal. This practice is discriminatory against the innovative companies.

Lastly, Canada has failed to ratify the WIPO Copyright and the WIPO Performances and Phonograms Treaties, resulting in Canada falling below global standards of copyright.

As mentioned, 2014 will present many opportunities for the United States, Canada, and Mexico to further improve their IP environments. As the committee is well aware, the TPP is being negotiated between 12 countries, and it is essential that it include a robust IP chapter. We would also encourage the Canadian Government to work closely with the business community to address specific IP issues within and outside the TPP and NAFTA frameworks and to raise their IP standards to levels consistent with the United States, the U.K., and Australia.

Thank you once again for the opportunity to testify.

Mr. SALMON. Thank you.

[The prepared statement of Mr. Elliot follows:]

# Statement
# of the
# U.S. Chamber
# of Commerce

**ON:**    NAFTA at Twenty: Accomplishments, Challenges, and the Way Forward on Intellectual Property

**TO:**    U.S. House Committee on Foreign Affairs
Subcommittee on the Western Hemisphere

**BY:**    Mr. Mark Elliot, Executive Vice President, Global
Intellectual Property Center, U.S. Chamber of Commerce

**DATE:**    January 15, 2014

The U.S. Chamber of Commerce is the world's largest business federation representing the interests of more than 3 million businesses of all sizes, sectors, and regions, as well as state and local chambers and industry associations. The Chamber is dedicated to promoting, protecting, and defending America's free enterprise system.

More than 96% of Chamber member companies have fewer than 100 employees, and many of the nation's largest companies are also active members. We are therefore cognizant not only of the challenges facing smaller businesses, but also those facing the business community at large.

Besides representing a cross-section of the American business community with respect to the number of employees, major classifications of American business—e.g., manufacturing, retailing, services, construction, wholesalers, and finance—are represented. The Chamber has membership in all 50 states.

The Chamber's international reach is substantial as well. We believe that global interdependence provides opportunities, not threats. In addition to the American Chambers of Commerce abroad, an increasing number of our members engage in the export and import of both goods and services and have ongoing investment activities. The Chamber favors strengthened international competitiveness and opposes artificial U.S. and foreign barriers to international business.

Positions on issues are developed by Chamber members serving on committees, subcommittees, councils, and task forces. Nearly 1,900 businesspeople participate in this process.

## Introduction

- Thank you Chairman Salmon and Ranking Member Sires.

- The U.S. Chamber of Commerce appreciates your leadership and the opportunity to testify today on the North American Free Trade Agreement on its twentieth anniversary.

- My name is Mark Elliot. I am the Executive Vice President of the U.S. Chamber of Commerce's Global Intellectual Property Center.

- Today, I am going to focus my testimony on intellectual property matters in regard to NAFTA, and Canada and Mexico specifically.

- As you know, the U.S. Chamber of Commerce's views on NAFTA are both wide-ranging and extensive, and my testimony today is intended to address only a narrow sub-section of the Chamber's overall perspective on NAFTA. The Chamber plans to submit broad comments encompassing all aspects of the NAFTA relationship to the Committee for review as well.

- In discussing the importance of protecting and enforcing intellectual property rights throughout the North American region, it is unfortunately necessary to highlight some concerns industry has, particularly in Canada.

## Importance of IP

- First, it is important to note the critical role intellectual property plays in creating jobs and spurring innovation.

- According to the U.S. Department of Commerce, U.S. IP industries account for:
  - $5 trillion of the nation's GDP;
  - 60 percent of exports; and
  - 40 million jobs;

- In short, intellectual property drives knowledge economies.

NAFTA and Rising International IP Standards

- At the time of its signing, NAFTA intended to create the best levels of IP protection and enforcement ever negotiated. It was a testament to how important IP was viewed by Mexico, Canada, and the United States.

- However, as this was signed twenty years ago, this level of IP protection is now a very low bar in 2014.

- Since NAFTA, IP protections and enforcement have continually improved around the globe, now making the IP provisions of NAFTA outdated. Standards in agreements such as the Korea-U.S. Free Trade Agreement are providing greater opportunity for trade.

- Even with the low bar set by NAFTA, we continue to see challenges in both Mexico and Canada on IP protections and enforcement.

IP Index highlights challenges specifically in Mexico and Canada

- Last December, the Chamber released an International IP Index, a comprehensive review of the intellectual property environment in 11 key markets based on existing international standards and best practices.

- Both Canada and Mexico's respective scores put them clearly in the second tier of countries, well below the developed-country standard, and markedly inconsistent with the competitiveness agendas both countries are advancing in other areas.

- With the highest possible score of 25, the likes of the United States, UK, and Australia performed well, receiving scores between 24 and 21. However, Mexico received a 12.2 and Canada received a mere 14.2, which actually puts its IP policies and enforcement closer to Russia, Malaysia, and even China.

- Mexico's low score is due to its relatively weak copyright protection, particularly online piracy, and the lack of IP enforcement and effective enforcement practices.

- We continue to see progress in Mexico, and we are working with the Mexican government on issues such as illegal camcording, implementing the World Intellectual Property Organization (WIPO) Internet Treaties and liability issues related to internet service providers (ISPs). In addition, Mexico is taking steps to provide regulatory data protection (RDP) for pharmaceuticals and providing a transparent pathway for patent linkage.

- As a whole, the business community is working productively with Mexico to improve its IP environment.

- Canada also scored low on the GIPC Index— in enforcement, particularly on effective border measures, but also scored weak on membership and ratification of international treaties and scored fairly low in both patents and copyrights.

- However, industry is expressing serious concerns about the IP environment in Canada.

- Canada is the largest trading partner for the United States—the bilateral trade totaled $582.4 billion a year, the equivalent of $1.6 billion a day in goods. U.S. exports to Canada totaled $277 billion per year, and as mentioned earlier, IP-industries account for 60% of U.S. exports. This makes it all the more bewildering to the business community at how substandard Canada's IP system is.

- In a recent op-ed in the Ottawa Citizen, Robert Atkinson, a Canadian and President of the Information Technology and Innovation Foundation (ITIF) and Michelle Wein, Trade Policy Analyst with ITIF called Canada "one of the leading nations in the world. And yet, surprisingly, Canada has a long tradition of providing intellectual property protections on a level with that of the developing world."

- I would like to provide a few specific examples of these industry concerns:

**(1) Patent Utility**: The WTO Agreement on Trade-Related Aspects of Intellectual Property Rights (TRIPS) and the North America Free Trade Agreement (NAFTA) require patents to be granted for inventions that are new, non-obvious, and useful, also known as "utility." This is not intended to be a burdensome requirement. It is simply to ensure that patents are not granted for inoperable, fanciful, or purely aesthetic inventions.

- Over the past eight years, approximately twenty pharmaceutical patents have been revoked in Canada for what is called "lack of utility or usefulness.
- This trend, which is not happening elsewhere in the world, is due to Canadian courts requiring evidence that is wholly inappropriate for judicial review of patent approvals, and it is a top concern for innovative pharmaceutical companies looking to do business in Canada.
  - For example, Indiana's Eli Lilly had a patent overturned under this patent utility umbrella, costing the innovative company $500 million in lost revenue. The same patent has been upheld everywhere it has been challenged.
- Canada is the only place patents have been routinely challenged solely on utility grounds.

**(2) Ex Officio**: Canada has yet to provide *ex officio* authority to its Customs officials to allow for the seizure of counterfeit and pirated products at the border. Instead, customs officials can seize suspected counterfeit goods only if 1) a court order is obtained by the trademark owner authorizing Customs to stop the goods; or 2) a directive is provided to Customs by the Royal Canadian Mounted Police (RCMP).

- We understand pending legislation in the Canadian Parliament addresses this, and we urge its swift passage.
- As former Canadian Ambassador to the United States Derek Burney has written, it is more difficult to transport a used mattress across the border strapped to the top of your car than it is to import a trunk-load of counterfeit software, DVDs or running shoes, which are not prohibited goods. Why? The mattress is deemed a health and safety risk under Canadian law unless it is certified to have been properly cleaned and fumigated. Believe it or not, Canadian border officials have no such authority independently to seize counterfeit goods.

**(3) Illicit Goods**: We continue to view with alarm the ongoing and substantial illicit trafficking in goods across some segments of the United States- Canada border. Recent reports estimate that the trade in counterfeit (and pirated) goods is as much as $600 billion.

- Counterfeiting and piracy in Canada are worth approximately $20 to 30 billion annually. These include sporting goods, medicines and personal care products, consumer electronics, pharmaceuticals, automotive parts, apparel, the list goes on. These goods may or may not be safe; they are clearly not regulated and not taxed.

- o This dangerous situation only serves to enrich organized criminals at the expense, in many instances, of public security, safety, and brand owners. Greater efforts need to be undertaken by both Canadian and U.S. authorities to address this illegal activity.

**(4) No Right of Appeal**: Due to Canada's regulations a patent owner, unlike a generic drug producer, does not have a right to appeal a Court decision. Following a decision by the Court in the first instance in favor of the generic producer, an appeal filed by the patent owner becomes moot. On the other hand, the right of appeal is available to the generic producer if the patent owner prevails in the first instance.

**(5) Copyright Protection**: Canada has also failed to ratify the WIPO Copyright Treaty (WCT) and WIPO Performances and Phonograms Treaty (WPPT),

- It is important to note that the recent signing of the Comprehensive and Economic and Trade Agreement (CETA) between the EU and Canada provides Canada with the opportunity to greatly improve its IP environment, particularly when it comes to pharmaceuticals.

- We encourage Canada to implement the CETA agreement appropriately and amend legislation and regulations accordingly.

2014 IP Index and TPP

- Later this month, the GIPC will be releasing the second edition of the International IP Index, with updated scores for the U. S., Canada, and Mexico.

- The Index will show that while progress has been made, there is still much more work to be done. Progress in Canada pertains to the improvements outlined in the CETA agreement and recognize the changes in Canada's Copyright law.

Opportunities for Improvement

- 2014 will present many opportunities for the United States, Canada, and Mexico to further improve their IP environments.

- As always, all three countries have the ability to pass legislation to ensure IP is better protected and enforced – and all three countries certainly have areas where they can improve.

- In particular, all three countries are participants in the Trans Pacific Partnership (TPP) Agreement negotiations.

- The TPP is being negotiated between 12 different countries, and it is essential that it include robust standards for IP protection, using the Korea-U.S. free trade agreement as a model and providing 12 years of regulatory data protection for biologic products.

- It has been reported that there is currently a proposal being discussed among the TPP negotiating countries that links a nation's income level to whether it will be required to provide IP protections to pharmaceuticals. This sends the wrong message that IP protection and enforcement only helps high-income countries and is a hindrance to low-and-middle income countries, and the Chamber is very concerned about this proposal. If this model applies more broadly, it is conceivable that some countries may never be required to respect global IP standards.

- We encourage the U.S., Canadian, Mexican, and all TPP negotiators to uphold their positions and protect IP from the efforts to weaken existing laws and norms.

- The TPP provides the U.S., Canada, and Mexico the opportunity to stand shoulder-to-shoulder in support of strong IP protections, innovation, and access to the creations and inventions of the 21$^{st}$ century.

- A TPP agreement that includes a high-standard IP chapter is good for jobs and good for international trade. The TPP will also allow Canada to raise its IP standards, promote innovation, and bolster its growing economy.

- 2014 should be the year when the North American neighbors work together to improve each other's IP environments and the IP environments of countries around the world.

- We thank the Subcommittee for holding his hearing, and we look forward to working with you to address those IP concerns on the North American continent.

———————

Mr. SALMON. Dr. Wood.

## STATEMENT OF DUNCAN WOOD, PH.D., DIRECTOR, MEXICO IN-STITUTE, WOODROW WILSON INTERNATIONAL CENTER FOR SCHOLARS

Mr. WOOD. Thank you, Mr. Chairman. Great pleasure to be here.

I always like to say that I am the perfect NAFTA citizen. I lived and was educated in Canada. I then moved to Mexico to work for 17 years. I then have moved here to the United States. I have a Canadian ex-wife, not because of any intellectual property dispute that we had. My children were born in Mexico but live in Canada. And I am now married to American and am living and working here. But I am a citizen of none of the three countries. So I guess that makes me the perfect person to comment.

A lot has been said about the success of NAFTA. I would like to talk about the potential of the North American region and what we need to do to realize that potential.

I think that we see four main factors in the potential for North America. The fully integrated production platform is something that we have talked about at great length already, and I think we need to emphasize that. It is very, very important to see that we are unique in the world in the way that industry in the three countries works together.

The second factor has already been mentioned, energy. North America's incredible energy abundance, from the massive hydro-electric resources and oil sands of Canada to the huge oil and gas reserves of the Gulf of Mexico, shale gas and tight oil fields on shore, and the world-class wind, solar, and geothermal resources of Mexico and the United States, means that the region's energy security is guaranteed for the foreseeable future.

But it is the cost of energy that gives us the real advantage in the world. The shale gas revolution has meant that gas prices and, therefore, the cost of electricity are incredibly low by international standards, conferring a huge boost to the cost-efficiency of North American manufacturing.

The third factor is human capital. North America has a demographic profile that gives it a significant long-term advantage over Europe, China, and Japan. The openness of Canada and the United States to immigration has allowed these countries to maintain a steady supply of young people who provide a workforce that satisfy labor needs.

Mexico's traditionally higher fertility rate has meant that it has been a source country for many of these young people, but its changing demographic pattern now means that it will produce less migrants than in years gone by. So we have to take advantage of the demographic bonus while it exists. The challenge is how do we invest in the region's young people.

The final factor is the internal market. We have 460 million people in the North American economic space, and their spending power combined exceeds that of any other nation or region. Total North American GDP will rise from $19 trillion today to over $50 trillion by 2050, when the regional population is forecast to top 630 million and Mexico is projected to be one of the world's five largest economies.

Mexico, with its relatively young population, a rising middle class, and with economic growth rates expected to surpass those in Canada and the United States, will generate the lion's share of North American growth. This will ensure that the domestic market in North America remains the most important in the world, even after Chinese GDP outgrows that of the United States.

So what do we need to do to guarantee the economic future?

First, we need to modernize and deepen North American integration. As has been mentioned here, NAFTA was a first-generation trade agreement signed in another era. We need to update it to take into consideration all of the new products that have been mentioned here. We need to strengthen our already considerable attributes if the region is going to be able to compete against other countries and regions of the world. Harmonizing regulations and standards, introducing agreements on services, and coordinating economic policy more closely will do just that.

Second, we must invest in our people to ensure that employers have the human talent they need to remain competitive. We need to give them the freedom to move in the region.

Third, we need to invest in our borders, in both infrastructure and in procedures, to ensure that integrated production processes in the region are efficient, agile, and competitive.

Fourth, we need to invest in energy infrastructure so that we create a fully integrated North American energy market that will ensure supply and keep prices low.

Finally, we need to think about how a strong North America can best engage with the rest of the world.

The potential of the TPP is considerable, but the negotiations must take into consideration the interests, strengths, and weaknesses of all three NAFTA partners. This means that we have to think not only about those who win from openness and free trade but also those who lose. How do we compensate those who lose their jobs or whose businesses cannot compete in a globalized economy? Though it is a thorny issue, this question must be answered adequately if we are to maintain political support for free markets, trade, and investment.

I am an optimist on this one, and I agree with Fred Bergsten, who has estimated that the benefits to the U.S. economy of 50 years of free trade equal around $1 trillion in annual GDP and that the benefits outweigh the cost by about 20 to 1.

Now is the moment for the United States, Mexico, and Canada to celebrate open regionalism and to take the necessary measures to make sure that our shared regional economy is strong enough to compete on the world stage. The TPP is one path, but we must recognize that there are also encouraging signs at last from the World Trade Organization after 12 years of stagnation. If we take the necessary measures, we cannot only enjoy a more prosperous future but also offer an example that the rest of the world may follow.

Thank you very much.

Mr. SALMON. Thank you very much.

[The prepared statement of Mr. Wood follows:]

Testimony given by Dr Duncan Wood, Director, Mexico Institute, to the

Subcommittee Hearing: NAFTA at Twenty: Accomplishments, Challenges, and the Way Forward

Subcommittee on the Western Hemisphere

2172 House Rayburn Office Building Washington, DC 20515 | Jan 15, 2014 2:00pm

Thank you, Mr. Chairman. Chairman Salmon, Ranking Member Sires, members of the committee, it is a privilege to join you today. I appreciate the invitation.

At the Mexico Institute in particular, and the Wilson Center more generally, we have worked a great deal on the development of North America, its successes and challenges. Recently, I partnered with Laura Dawson (of Dawson Strategic) and Christopher Sands (of the Hudson Institute) to defend the concept of North America and to call for an ambitious plan for the future. In "North American Competitiveness: The San Diego Agenda" we put forward the idea that,

> "we must deepen North American economic integration in order to compete more effectively globally. That means common regulations and standards on products manufactured in North America, negotiating as a bloc with the Asians and Europeans, making both borders function more efficiently, investing in physical infrastructure, supporting innovation and education, facilitating labor mobility, and aligning our energy policies."[i]

Twenty years after its formation, the North American Free Trade Agreement (NAFTA) remains a useful, if incomplete, expression of the economic ties between these three countries. It has also proven itself to be of great importance in partially achieving the full economic potential of the North American region. In order to provide a balanced and fair assessment of the NAFTA at this time, I feel it is important to ask 3 basic questions:

1. What was the goal of the agreement when it was negotiated?
2. What is the potential of the region today?
3. What is missing to fully realize the potential of today's North America?

In many ways, we can see the NAFTA as a first generation regional free trade agreement, designed in the context of the end of the Cold War, an international trading regime in crisis, and of great concerns about the contemporary and future competitiveness of the U.S. economy. The agreement was designed to liberalize trade between the three North American nations, to improve competitiveness, and to increase levels of foreign direct investment. Many people have since associated other goals with the agreement. For example, some have argued that NAFTA was supposed to reduce or end the massive migration of Mexicans to the United States by creating jobs in Mexico. However, although the NAFTA has created hundreds of thousands of jobs throughout the region, and Mexico-U.S. migration has now fallen to the level where we can say it is net-zero, this was never an official goal of the agreement.

People also criticize the NAFTA for job losses in the United States, Canada and Mexico. It is certainly true that U.S. manufacturing found it increasingly difficult in the 1980s, 90s and 2000s to remain competitive as emerging markets became an integral part of the global trading system. In particular, the emergence of China as a major exporting nation has posed a serious challenge to the manufactured goods export competitiveness of the United States, Mexico and Canada but we can point to the rise of a number of other new exporting powers as threatening U.S. and regional competitiveness.

However, we can make a convincing case that, through the NAFTA, U.S. manufacturers have been able to maintain competitiveness by importing parts and components from developing countries, thereby lowering their cost structure. And this is one of the most important elements that is all too often ignored about NAFTA: U.S. manufacturers were able to keep skilled jobs in the United States by importing parts and components from other countries. Openness has been good for the U.S. economy: according to Fred Bergsten, in a presentation at the Wilson Center last week, the US economy is $1 trillion better off as a result of integration with the world economy over the past 50 years, and he estimates a benefit-cost ratio of 20-1 from free trade.

And this is where Mexico and Canada have played a central role. The NAFTA countries used to trade goods with each other but, in the words of my Mexico Institute colleague, Chris Wilson, now they "build them together". Today the integration of the manufacturing systems across the North American region has meant that imports from NAFTA partners into the United States in fact involve the repatriation of value that originated in the United States. In the case of Canadian imports into the U.S., 25% of their value, on average, originated in America; in the case of Mexican imports, that figure is 40%. Compare this with only 4% in goods imported from China. By harnessing the comparative advantage of all three economies into one integrated system, North America is able to compete effectively in the global economy, and has been able to maintain value-adding activities in the United States. Importing goods from Mexico and Canada helps to promote jobs in the United States by comparison with importing from any other region of the world.

In fact, it can be argued that the NAFTA, although it was a less ambitious agreement than some of the models that have marked international trade negotiations since 1994, hit the "sweet spot" by providing enough liberalization to allow for growth in trade and investment, and the integration of production processes between the three countries, without creating supranational institutions of the European kind that have been shown to be highly problematical in recent years.

As for the potential of North America today, we can see it in four main factors. The first, a fully integrated production platform has already been mentioned. This factor will continue to be crucial in ensuring regional competitiveness into the future. The second factor is energy. North America's incredible natural endowments, from the massive hydroelectric resources and oil sands of Canada, to the huge oil and gas reserves of the Gulf of Mexico, the shale gas and tight oil fields onshore, and the world class wind, solar and geothermal resources of Mexico and the US, means that the region's energy security is guaranteed for the foreseeable future. However, it is the cost of energy that has come to be of central importance in determining North American competitiveness today. The shale gas revolution has meant that gas prices and the cost of electricity generation are remarkably low by international standards, conferring a huge boost to the cost efficiency of North American manufacturing. It is this factor that has been responsible for the return of manufacturing to the United States in recent years, and the recent reforms in Mexico should allow the same process to occur there.

The third factor is human capital. North America has a demographic profile that gives it a significant long-term advantage over Europe, China and Japan. The openness of Canada and the United States to immigration has allowed those countries to maintain a steady supply of young people who provide a workforce that can satisfy labor needs. Mexico's traditionally higher fertility rate has meant that it has been a source country for many of these young people, but its changing demographic pattern now means that it will produce less migrants than in years gone by. The challenge in all three countries is now to invest in this human capital through education and training, and to allow for greater mobility of workers to satisfy the labor needs of the region as a whole. With Mexico producing more engineers every year than the United States, the opportunity seems obvious, but we must also invest in the education and training of software engineers, doctors, managers, plumbers, mechanics and technicians of all kinds. This would be best done in a coordinated fashion between the governments, private sectors and educational institutions of the three countries.

The final factor is also related to population size and the internal market. The 460 million people of the North American economic space have a spending power that far exceeds that of any other nation or region. Total North American GDP will rise from $19 trillion today to over $50 trillion by 2050, when regional population is forecast to top 630 million and Mexico is projected to be one of the world's five largest economies. Mexico, with its relatively young population, a rising middle class, and with economic growth rates expected to surpass those in Canada and the U.S., will generate the lion's share of the North American growth. This will ensure that the "domestic" market in North America remains the most important in the world, even after Chinese GDP outgrows that of the U.S..

What is needed now, then, to secure the economic future? First, we need to modernize and deepen North American integration. As mentioned above, NAFTA was completed in 1994 and was a first-generation trade agreement, before our economies and our lives came to be dominated by things such as smart phones, tablets, biotech, e-commerce or fracking. In the intervening period, and largely thanks to the NAFTA, industry has developed integrated, just-in-time supply chains across borders. We must strengthen our already considerable attributes if the region is to be able to compete against other countries and regions of the world. This means continuing to harmonize regulations and standards, and to coordinate economic policy more closely between the three partners.

Second, we must invest in our people to ensure that employers have the human resources they need to remain competitive and we need to give them the freedom to move in the region. Third, we need to invest our borders, in both infrastructure and in procedures, to ensure that the integrated production process in the region is efficient, agile and competitive. Fourth, we need to invest in energy infrastructure so that we create a fully integrated North American energy market that will ensure supply and keep prices low.

Finally, we need to think about how a strong North America can best engage with the rest of the world. The potential of the Trans Pacific Partnership is considerable, but the negotiations must take into consideration the interests, strengths and weakness of all three NAFTA partners. This means that we have to think not only about those who win from openness and free trade, but also those who lose. How do we compensate those who lose their jobs, or whose businesses cannot compete in a globalized economy? Though thorny, this question must be answered adequately if we are to maintain political support for free markets, trade and investment.

Now is the moment for the United States, Mexico and Canada to celebrate open regionalism and to take the necessary measures to make sure that our shared regional economy is strong enough to compete on the world stage. The TPP is one path but we must recognize that there are also encouraging signs at last from the World Trade Organization (WTO), after 12 years of stagnation. If we take the necessary measures, we can not only enjoy a more prosperous future, but also offer an example that the rest of the world may follow.

---

[i] Charles Shapiro, Prologue, *North American Competitiveness: The San Diego Agenda*, by Laura Dawson, Christopher Sands and Duncan Wood.

Mr. SALMON. I am going to recess the subcommittee so that we can go vote on the floor, and we will be back to ask questions. Thank you.

[Recess.]

Mr. SALMON. We will reconvene the subcommittee. And I would like to start off the questioning first with Mr. Farnsworth.

How has NAFTA affected the trade balance between the three countries? How do energy imports affect the trade balance? And will Mexico's energy reforms have implications for the trade in energy?

Mr. FARNSWORTH. Well, thank you, sir, for the opportunity.

The trade balance is a factor of many things, not just NAFTA. And so a lot of times people say, well, after we passed NAFTA, the trade balance changed overnight almost, it seemed, in 1994. That was a result of the peso crisis, et cetera. So, at one level, it is a difficult linkage to make. What NAFTA did was it opened up both economies to each other.

Clearly, energy is actually a part of that. And one of the things that we often hear in terms of NAFTA as a criticism is that the U.S. trade balance with Mexico has changed into the negative. A lot of that has to do with the fact that, frankly, we are importing energy from Mexico. We are also importing a lot, obviously, from Canada, which is our number-one supplier of energy. And so those energy relationships would occur with or without NAFTA. So I think we just have to be a little bit careful there in that context.

But as energy reforms go through in Mexico, we think this is a game-changer for several reasons. Number one is because—we have talked a little bit about the cost of energy. Energy right now in Mexico, electricity in particular, is really expensive. And from a manufacturing perspective, that is a very important input. As the cost of energy decreases, manufacturing is going to be a lot more competitive, and that builds into the entire idea we have all been talking about about North America as a production platform. But you are also going to have huge opportunities for U.S. investors, for the first time since 1938, to have the opportunity, perhaps, to work directly with the Mexican energy sector.

And you are also going to have opportunities for U.S. technology and U.S. capital to be deployed. And this is really important because, particularly in the context of natural gas, which Mexico has an awful lot of but hasn't been able to develop because they haven't had the technology and capital, these are, in some ways, environmentally sensitive issues, and you have to have best practices, you have to have cutting-edge technology, you have to know what you are doing, or else you can really make a mess of things. That is U.S. technology. The U.S. is in the lead here. And so to deploy that technology in the Mexican energy sector we think is a very good thing.

So that is going to contribute very directly to the trade balance because, frankly, those are exports. Also, I have to say that will also contribute to Canada's trade balance. Those will be exports from Canada, too. Canada has a very robust energy sector.

I would very quickly also just align myself with your comments about the XL Pipeline. I think that is a very important thing.

And I also want to congratulate Congress, in fact, as well, on moving forward with the transboundary hydrocarbon agreement with Mexico.

Mr. SALMON. Thank you very much.

Mr. Elliot, as I mentioned earlier, I have some grave concerns about some of the IP infractions in Canada. And you focused a large part of your testimony on the same issue. I find it very disconcerting that they have appeared on USTR's watchlist that singles out countries where IPR is inconsistent. Really consistently, for the last 20 years, they have been on that list.

What is the best mechanism for us to try to address it? To me, it is a very, very serious concern. And if we are going to look at new trade agreements, maybe that is where they should be raised. Or should they be maybe raised through the existing trade agreement? What are your thoughts? Because I am not going to let it go.

Thank you.

Mr. ELLIOT. Sure. And thank you, Chairman Salmon, for not letting it go. It is a very important issue to the business community.

I think there are a couple of parts to this. If you break out the patent utility piece itself, you know, there are a number of different ways you can tackle that one. If the Canadian Government don't see an obligation through NAFTA to fix it, then certainly you would imagine there is an obligation through the EU-Canada CETA agreement to fix it. If not, there will certainly be through the TPP. And if not, you know, it has been spelled out over a number of years through the Special 301 process; it is quite clear what the problem is.

The frustrating aspect of this is that in the U.S., Europe, and Canada the law is virtually the same. There is just a very minor clause in there which makes the difference. And in the U.S. and Europe, it is defining the area as capable of industrial application. And the Canadian law says "lack of utility." There are the differences in the wording of the legislation. It is a relatively easy fix.

My view is that, you know, there are a number of different mechanisms here to put some pressure on the Canadian Government to act on this. I would hope that the Canadian Government would see the need to address it for their own purposes, and, quite simply, it is the right thing to do.

Mr. SALMON. I find it kind of incredulous that some of these Canadian generic companies would want to offer a product that has no utility.

Mr. ELLIOT. Yes, indeed. I mean, part of the irony here is, of course, if the court finds that the patent has no utility, then of course the generic entrant enters the market, proving of course there was utility after all.

Mr. SALMON. Mr. Sires.

Mr. SIRES. I guess that is how they keep the cost of medicine down.

You know, in your statement, Mr. Elliot, you said that China sends the counterfeit through Canada, through here. And how much was it that you estimate a year that comes to the United States through Canada?

Mr. ELLIOT. There is somewhere between $20 billion and $30 billion a year in the counterfeit business running through Canada at the moment.

Mr. SIRES. And that just gets passed on to us?

Mr. ELLIOT. Not all of it. Not all of it. Some of that would. Some would remain in Canada.

Mr. SIRES. Yeah, obviously.

Mr. ELLIOT. Yeah.

Mr. SIRES. But a lot of it comes to us.

Mr. ELLIOT. That is correct.

Mr. SIRES. What about our border checks or anything like that? That doesn't come into play?

Mr. ELLIOT. Yeah. There are a couple of aspects on this. I mean, I think there is an issue around the counterfeits entering Canada, and I think that is the ex officio issue here, where the law enforcement people don't have the authority without a court order to seize goods coming through.

There was a former Canadian Ambassador to the United States who wrote that it is more difficult to transport a used mattress across the border on top of your car than a truckload of counterfeit products into the U.S. And there is some truth in that. Look, and some of this is, of course, not solely on Canada.

Mr. SIRES. Right.

Mr. ELLIOT. There is an issue here on the U.S. side.

But part of the frustration here, I think, is that, to some extent, the Canadian Government is not inspecting some of the materials coming from China that they believe are en route to the U.S. And then, of course, when it enters the U.S., the U.S. authorities are perhaps not applying the same sort of attention to it, feeling that it is coming from Canada and, therefore, not requiring the same level of attention as it would if it were coming directly from China.

Mr. SIRES. Dr. Wood, how do labor and environment provisions in recent free-trade agreements and reportedly in the TPP differ from those of NAFTA?

Mr. WOOD. Thank you.

I think we are in a crucial moment in the TPP negotiations, where we are seeing the pushback on certain environmental and labor negotiations.

We were fortunate enough within NAFTA to be able to create these side agreements that actually did help to raise standards, in Mexico in particular. We also developed an institution at the border, the North American Development Bank, that sought to develop the border region in an environmentally safe way to improve drinking water, paving. Now they are moving on into renewable energy and emissions, which are very, very important features of industrialization.

That was something which was added into the NAFTA sort of after the fact, after the negotiations, but it became a crucial element. And I think we probably could do a lot more on that in NAFTA.

What I am concerned about with TPP is that we need to make sure that those standards remain high. And as the piece that was published in the New York Times this morning highlighted, at the moment it seems as though the United States is backing off from an insistence on high environmental and labor standards in that agreement.

It is an issue that is important not just in the sense of protecting jobs here but also in making sure that the development of those countries—because, ultimately, that is what we are looking for. We are looking for the development of those markets around the Pacific Basin as an outlet for U.S. goods. Their development needs to be sustainable in every sense of the word.

And so I think that is the concern that needs to be there front and center. It needs to be an issue that U.S. negotiators have a strong stance on.

Mr. SIRES. Thank you.

Mr. Farnsworth, how come we have such large deficits with some of these countries and we have this trade agreement?

Mr. FARNSWORTH. Well, again, sir, it is a really good question because it is asked all the time. And the deficit itself is an accounting mechanism that isn't necessarily linked directly to trade agreements or not. I mean, this is a much broader number, if you will, and it is the flip side of investment numbers, et cetera, et cetera, as you would note from economics.

But, having said that, what trade agreements have done, and it was said in the previous panel, is opened foreign markets that were previously closed to the United States in a way that is done on a reciprocal basis. And this is oftentimes really important because the United States has generally given unilateral trade preferences to our trade partners traditionally. And the trade agreements, actually, what they do is they give us equal access to those foreign markets that we haven't had in the past.

And so, if we want to increase our exports, we have to find ways to open new markets. And that is precisely what we have seen, at least in the Western Hemisphere, where I know the stories much better, in terms of bilateral agreements with Chile, the bilateral agreements with Peru, the bilateral agreement with Colombia, with CAFTA, the Central American countries. And it is also what we have seen in terms of NAFTA.

Now, the issue with Mexico right after the agreement went into force was—again, I mentioned it very briefly—but the peso devaluation, which changed the terms of trade. But that wasn't specifically related to NAFTA. In fact, it was NAFTA that locked Mexico in to a course of activity that prevented them from doing things that they might have done previously, as they did in the 1980s, to close their markets. And what NAFTA did is they kept those markets open. And as a direct result, Mexico returned to global capital markets in a matter of months, whereas during the crisis of the 1980s it took them years to get back.

So, in fact, NAFTA was a framework that really helped contain the damage but also gave Mexico a ladder to get out of it. Now, that doesn't guarantee that every policy action every country takes is going to be favorable or not have negative consequences or, frankly, that the trade agreement is going to be able to ameliorate every bad thing that happens. But that is one way to look at some of these issues, and I think a very helpful way.

Mr. SIRES. Our latest trade agreement with Colombia, how is that working? Anyone want to——

Mr. WOOD. Yeah. I mean, the information that I have on the trade agreement with Colombia is that it is working quite well for the United States but not so well for Colombian exporters. They haven't been able to take advantage of the terms of that agreement in the same way as the United States has. And it is——

Mr. SIRES. They also signed a trade agreement with Canada, right, totaling $7 billion?

Mr. WOOD. I believe they did, yes.

Mr. SIRES. They have. So——

Mr. WOOD. But I think that one thing is that we are at the fortunate point of view or perspective of 20 years of NAFTA. We can look back. The free-trade agreement with Colombia is still relatively new. They take time to mature. And I think adopting a longer-term historical perspective is crucial in this question.

Just as with your question to Eric Farnsworth just now. Mexico is on this development path where ultimately their terms of trade are going to change. They will start to import a lot more from the United States, just as they have done already. We have seen the transformation of the Mexican economy. So they import a lot more than they used to. And trade matters a lot more to Mexico than it did 20 years ago. Back then, trade as a percentage of GDP was at 30 percent. Now we are looking at 70 percent of GDP related to trade. That is a huge transformation for the country.

Mr. FARNSWORTH. If I can make just a very quick comment on Colombia to add to what Duncan was saying.

The real winner in terms of the Colombia trade agreement has been the United States, because, again, this was an agreement that—Colombia had unilateral free market access into the United States through the original Andean Trade Preference Act from 1991. That was later extended and expanded into the ATPDEA in the year 2000. But that was always unilateral access that the Colombians enjoyed into the United States. What the U.S. didn't have was reciprocal access into Colombia, and that is what the FTA has granted us.

Now, the Colombian FTA has only been in operation for a short period of time. And it always gives me a chuckle when you hear the opponents of trade agreements particularly talk about difficulties in, for example, the Colombian agriculture sector and they blame the trade agreement with the United States. But the terms of implementation of the agriculture provisions in the trade agreement haven't gone into effect yet because they have been backloaded in terms of transition periods, just like we did with NAFTA, over a 15-year period. So you get all these complaints sometimes about agreements, when, in fact, the agreement isn't even operative in those sectors.

So Colombia, I think, is a country that we are going to see increasing dynamism. And what the exciting thing has been for that particular country is they are actually seeing the trade agreements with Canada and the United States and now with the Pacific Alliance and some of the interesting things they are doing in the Pacific not as the endpoint but as the beginning point, the access point to the global economy that then allows them to take the domestic reforms they need to on labor rights and on the environment and on education, on innovation, all the things we know so well, and use the trade agreement as really a spur to those broader national development goals.

And, ultimately, I think that is where the people of Colombia want to go, and I think that is where the United States would want them to go, as well.

Mr. SIRES. And the South Korea trade agreement, how is that doing?

Mr. FARNSWORTH. I am not an expert there, I am sorry.

Mr. SIRES. Okay.

Anybody?

Okay. Well, I guess we can end it on that.

Mr. SALMON. All right.

Well, that concludes our questions. We would really like to thank the second panel very much for taking your time. And sorry about the hiatus that we just had to endure, but thank you very, very much.

I don't have any other comments or questions. I am actually very, very encouraged that NAFTA has been a very, very phenomenal success and a success that we can build upon with other FTAs. So thank you very much.

And this hearing is concluded.

[Whereupon, at 4:40 p.m., the subcommittee was adjourned.]

# APPENDIX

---

62

**SUBCOMMITTEE HEARING NOTICE**
**COMMITTEE ON FOREIGN AFFAIRS**
U.S. HOUSE OF REPRESENTATIVES
WASHINGTON, DC 20515-6128

**Subcommittee on the Western Hemisphere**
**Matt Salmon (R-AZ), Chairman**

January 10, 2014

**TO:   MEMBERS OF THE COMMITTEE ON FOREIGN AFFAIRS**

You are respectfully requested to attend an OPEN hearing of the Subcommittee on the Western Hemisphere, to be held in Room 2172 of the Rayburn House Office Building (and available live on the Committee website at http://www.ForeignAffairs.house.gov):

**DATE:**          Wednesday, January 15, 2014

**TIME:**          2:00 p.m.

**SUBJECT:**     NAFTA at Twenty: Accomplishments, Challenges, and the Way Forward

**WITNESSES:**   Panel I
The Honorable Carla A. Hills
Chairman and Chief Executive Officer
Hills & Company International Consultants

The Honorable David Dreier
Chairman
Annenberg-Dreier Commission at Sunnylands

Panel II
Mr. Eric Farnsworth
Vice President
Council of the Americas and Americas Society

Mr. Mark T. Elliot
Executive Vice President
Global Intellectual Property Center
U.S. Chamber of Commerce

Duncan Wood, Ph.D.
Director
Mexico Institute
Woodrow Wilson International Center for Scholars

**By Direction of the Chairman**

# COMMITTEE ON FOREIGN AFFAIRS

MINUTES OF SUBCOMMITTEE ON _____ *the Western Hemisphere* _____ HEARING

Day __*Wednesday*__ Date __*01/15/2014*__ Room __*2172 RHOB*__

Starting Time __*2:36 p.m.*__ Ending Time __*4:38 p.m.*__

Recesses __*1*__ ( *4:02* to *4:24* ) (___to___) (___to___) (___to___) (___to___) (___to___)

Presiding Member(s)

*Chairman Matt Salmon*

Check all of the following that apply:

Open Session ☑  
Executive (closed) Session ☐  
Televised ☑

Electronically Recorded (taped) ☑  
Stenographic Record ☑

TITLE OF HEARING:

*"NAFTA at Twenty: Accomplishments, Challenges, and the Way Forward"*

SUBCOMMITTEE MEMBERS PRESENT:

*Chairman Matt Salmon, Ranking Member Albio Sires, Rep. Trey Radel, Rep. Gregory Meeks, Rep. Jeff Duncan, and Rep. Ron DeSantis.*

NON-SUBCOMMITTEE MEMBERS PRESENT: *(Mark with on * if they are not members of full committee.)*

*Chairman Ed Royce.*

HEARING WITNESSES: Same as meeting notice attached? Yes ☑ No ☐  
*(If "no", please list below and include title, agency, department, or organization.)*

STATEMENTS FOR THE RECORD: *(List any statements submitted for the record.)*

*Chairman Salmon - Statement for the Record of the Pharmaceutical Research and Manufacturers of America (PhRMA) to the Subcommittee on the Western Hemisphere of the House Committee on Foreign Affairs.*

TIME SCHEDULED TO RECONVENE _____  
or  
TIME ADJOURNED __*4:38 p.m.*__

Subcommittee Staff Director

MATERIAL SUBMITTED FOR THE RECORD BY THE HONORABLE MATT SALMON, A REP-
RESENTATIVE IN CONGRESS FROM THE STATE OF ARIZONA, AND CHAIRMAN, SUB-

950 F STREET, NW, SUITE 300 · WASHINGTON, DC 20004 · 202-835-3400 · PhRMA.org

# STATEMENT FOR THE RECORD
# OF THE PHARMACEUTICAL RESEARCH AND
# MANUFACTURERS OF AMERICA (PhRMA)

# TO THE

# HOUSE COMMITTEE ON FOREIGN AFFAIRS
# SUBCOMMITTEE ON
# THE WESTERN HEMISPHERE

## "NAFTA at Twenty: Accomplishments,
## Challenges, and the Way Forward"

## January 21, 2014

COMMITTEE ON THE WESTERN HEMISPHERE

We appreciate this Subcommittee's attention to the North American Free Trade Agreement's (NAFTA) successes and how the U.S. might learn from its experiences with that trade agreement to update its standards in ongoing trade negotiations. The hearing and the Subcommittee's ongoing work are important opportunities to discuss opportunities for improving our trading ties, as well as raise concerns about our NAFTA trading partners' intellectual property (IP) environments, especially that of Canada, which continues to be characterized by uncertainty and instability for U.S. innovative biopharmaceutical companies.

The Pharmaceutical Research and Manufacturers of America (PhRMA) is a nonprofit association that represents America's leading global pharmaceutical research and biotechnology companies which are devoted to inventing medicines that allow patients to live longer, healthier, and more productive lives. With nearly $50 billion invested in R&D in 2012,[1] and having produced more than half the world's new molecules in the last decade, our members are world leaders in medical research.[2] PhRMA represents a full spectrum of biopharmaceutical companies, ranging from large, global companies to smaller companies, all of which make valuable contributions to the health of patients and the economy. In fact, the U.S. innovative biopharmaceutical industry supported 3.4 million U.S. jobs and $789 billion in economic output (direct and indirect effects considered) in 2011,[3] and exported over $50 billion in biopharmaceuticals in 2012, making the sector the third largest U.S. exporter among R&D-intensive industries.[4]

## Canada

Canada lacks sufficient IP protections for innovative biopharmaceutical companies in several key respects. *First*, contrary to the Canadian Patent Act, Canada's treaty obligations under the World Trade Organization (WTO) Agreement on Trade-Related Aspects of Intellectual Property Rights (TRIPS), NAFTA, and established international norms, the Canadian judiciary has created a heightened standard for patentable utility. Canada's judicial "promise doctrine" creates a heightened patentability requirement for showing utility that is discriminatorily applied to biopharmaceutical products and raises uncertainty as to how much information needs to be disclosed in patent applications.

Specifically, innovators are now required to "demonstrate" or "soundly predict" the effectiveness of a pharmaceutical "promised" at the time of filing the patent application in Canada in order to meet the utility requirement. Such a standard is fundamentally inconsistent with TRIPS, as well as impracticable to meet due to the R&D timeline for pharmaceuticals. To satisfy the utility requirement, TRIPS, and all developed countries, require only that an invention be "useful" or "capable of industrial application." It is not reasonable or financially feasible to

---

[1] Pharmaceutical Research and Manufacturers of America. "PhRMA Annual Membership Survey." 1981–2013.
[2] Battelle Technology Partnership Practice. Growth Platform for Economics Around the World. Battelle Memorial Institute, May 2012. Prepared for the Pharmaceutical Research and Manufacturers of America.
[3] Battelle Technology Partnership Practice. The Economic Impact of the U.S. Biopharmaceutical Industry. July 2013. Battelle Memorial Institute. Prepared for the Pharmaceutical Research and Manufacturers of America.
[4] U.S. International Trade Commission. Trade DataWeb, accessed July 12, 2013, at http://dataweb.usitc.gov/ (query run of U.S. domestic exports classified by 4-digit NAIC code 3254).

require pharmaceutical firms to undertake substantial risks and spend millions of dollars on clinical drug development before a patent application is even filed. Canada's "promise doctrine" discourages the investment of significant resources to develop new medicines and, in the long run, negatively affects the patients and families who rely upon our sector to develop innovative medicines.

This issue undermines the ability of innovative biopharmaceutical companies to enforce and defend their existing patents in the court system and obtain new patents with the Canadian Intellectual Property Office (CIPO) for innovative cures and treatments. Standards for patentability in Canada should comport with Canada's international commitments and be applied in a neutral, non-discriminatory manner. That biopharmaceutical innovators should face significant intellectual property challenges with one of the largest trading partners to the U.S., EU, and Japan – and a developed country – is unacceptable.

*Second,* Canada's intellectual property regime currently provides no form of patent term restoration (PTR). Although Canada recently agreed in principle to adopt a form of PTR in the context of the Comprehensive Economic and Trade Agreement (CETA) with the European Union, concerns remain regarding the conditions and limitations within the agreed upon PTR mechanism. At a maximum period of two years, the proposed PTR period for Canada reached in CETA would be lower than the maximum of five years provided to patent owners in other developed nations, including the United States, the EU and Japan. In addition, it is reported that the proposed PTR mechanism could include an exception for Canadian-made generic drugs to be exported during the period of additional protection, which is not found in the United States' or any other nation's PTR mechanism and would undermine the value of patent rights.

Canada is one of the only industrialized countries not to provide any form of PTR to compensate for patent life lost due to delays in the regulatory approval process. The need for some form of PTR is compounded by the fact that Canada's regulatory approval process for new drugs generally takes longer than the equivalent U.S. approval process. Because of the significant time it takes to develop and obtain approval for a new biopharmaceutical product, the effective patent life for such a product is often substantially reduced. Regulatory approval delays, combined with the present lack of PTR, harm the ability of an innovator to realize an invention's full value.

*Third,* the Canadian Patented Medicines (Notice of Compliance) Regulations include several key deficiencies that weaken Canada's enforcement of patents, including the lack of effective right of appeal for patent owners. While Canada has stated that it will take action to address the right of appeal issue in the context of CETA, PhRMA members note that Canada also appears to be intent on making additional changes to its patent enforcement system that may remove or weaken other existing rights of patent owners.

The summary nature of Canada's initial patent infringement proceedings means that innovative biopharmaceutical manufacturers, unlike a generic drug producer, are not provided an effective right of appeal from adverse patent decisions, while such a right is afforded to generic companies. Canada's PM (NOC) Regulations provide that a generic product may be approved for marketing following a decision by the court in the first instance in favor of the generic producer; once approved, an appeal filed by the patent owner becomes moot. The patent owner is then left with no alternative but to start a new proceeding outside of the framework of the regulatory proceedings – in other words, an action for patent infringement once the generic product enters the market. Thus, the innovator must essential restart a case it had already spent up to two years litigating under the regulations.

In contrast, a right of appeal is available to the generic under the regulations if the patent owner prevails in the first instance. This creates an unfair advantage to generic manufacturers and creates a perverse incentive to challenge patents. The right of appeal issue is simply a matter of fairness and equality; all biopharmaceutical companies should be granted the equivalent appeal rights under the Canadian system.

*Finally*, PhRMA members continue to have serious concerns about the potential loss of regulatory data protection (RDP) under the relevant Canadian regulations if the innovator drug is not being marketed in Canada. Article 39.3 of the TRIPS Agreement and NAFTA Articles 1711(5) and (6) require Canadian regulatory authorities to provide effective protection to prevent the unfair commercial use of clinical trial and other data submitted by innovative companies for market approval of their products. Although Canada implemented eight years of RDP in October 2006, it imposes unfair and arbitrary limitations on the application of that RDP if an innovative medicine is not being marketed in Canada. Canada's obligation to protect data pursuant to the relevant TRIPS and NAFTA provisions is not in any way lessened simply because the approved medicine or vaccine is not marketed in Canada. Moreover, these restrictions have a serious adverse impact on the ability of U.S. innovative biopharmaceutical companies to protect from unfair commercial use the significant efforts and expenditures made in producing these data.

As Mr. Mark Elliot astutely noted at the January 15th hearing, Canada is the largest trading partner for the United States, with bilateral trade totaling $582.4 billion a year and U.S. exports to Canada totaling $277 billion per year. IP-intensive industries account for 60% of U.S. exports, and the U.S. research-based biopharmaceutical industry is the country's third largest export sector among those. It is unacceptable that Canada should enforce such significant market access barriers that hurt not only U.S. industry but Canadian patients as well. Strong IP protections are a critical element of an ecosystem that creates incentives for investment by our innovative industry in new treatments and cures for unmet patient needs. PhRMA urges this Subcommittee to continue to find opportunities to engage with Canada on improving its IP regime.

## Mexico

The U.S. innovative biopharmaceutical industry is also concerned about the lack of effective patent enforcement and insufficient RDP provisions in its other NAFTA partner, Mexico.

Mexico has taken steps toward the goal of eliminating unnecessary, costly, and time consuming court actions to obtain appropriate legal protection for innovative biopharmaceutical companies' patents, including a mechanism for the Mexican health regulatory agency, COFEPRIS, to consult patent listings in the Official Gazette before the issuance of marketing authorizations for generic products. Effective patent enforcement mechanisms inherently prevent the marketing of follow-on products when such marketing would infringe valid patent rights. Yet Mexico only provides effective patent enforcement for active chemical substantives rather than for product, formulation, and use patents as the United States provides.

Further, U.S. innovative biopharmaceutical companies continue to face challenges in removing patent infringing products from the marketplace. Obtaining effective preliminary injunctions or final decisions on cases regarding IP infringement within a reasonable time (as well as collecting adequate damages when appropriate) remain a rare exception rather than the norm. This is clearly inconsistent with Mexico's commitments under TRIPS and NAFTA.

Despite the commitments of COFEPRIS and Mexico's IP office, INPI, Mexico has not yet implemented substantive RDP. In June 2012, COFEPRIS issued guidelines to implement RDP for a period of not less than five years – an important step toward fulfilling Mexico's obligations under TRIPS and NAFTA. As guidelines, however, their validity may be questioned when applied to a concrete case, and they could be hard to enforce or revoked at any time. In addition, the apparent distinction made by the regulatory authorities between the provision of RDP to small and large molecule drugs creates significant uncertainty for the innovative biopharmaceutical industry. Consistent with TRIPS, RDP should be provided regardless of the manner in which the medicine is synthesized. The passage of regulations on RDP can provide greater clarity and confidence in Mexico's IP protections.

***

NAFTA was a ground-breaking trade agreement in its incorporation of IP provisions that supported and encouraged North American innovation. The United States and its NAFTA partners now stand on the brink of the next gold standard agreement – the Trans-Pacific Partnership (TPP). There is no question that strong IP provisions are fundamentally important to innovative biopharmaceutical member companies' ability to invest in the R&D for new medicines that is so costly in terms of time, human resources, and capital, and for which the risks are magnified at the cutting edge of biologics research. Creating the right environment for innovation in North America through robust IP regimes will not only boost high-value, high-skill job creation and our integrated economies overall, but will result in better outcomes for patients through the discovery and development of innovative medicines.